Angela F. Rawson, from Yorkshire, and Leicestershire-born Nikki Rowan-Kedge have been in business together for twenty-five years. They began as specialist caterers and their business grew into a unique restaurant, the Loaves and Fishes, where the food is homemade, wholesome, fresh, non-faddish and, of course, supremely delicious.

Angela Rawson has loved cooking since she was six years old. It was in the family: her great-aunt Iris Syrett founded the world-famous Tante Marie School of Cookery in the 1950s. Angela's cooking has featured in national newspapers and magazines, and this is the fourth book she and Nikki have written together.

The Loaves and Fishes restaurant is at East Sands, Burbage, Marlborough, Wiltshire; telephone 01672 810211. The photographs for the book were taken in the restaurant.

ACKNOWLEDGEMENTS

Many thanks to the friends and supporters of the Loaves and Fishes restaurant. To Harry Dodson for his wonderful vegetables, fruit, flowers and herbs from the gardens of Chilton Manor. To Mr and Mrs Vallis for the beautiful roses featured on the cover, and for the restaurant flowers during the summer months. Thanks also to our editor, Mari Roberts, for her patience and guidance in putting this book together.

Also by Angela F. Rawson and Nikki Rowan-Kedge:

Wiltshire Cookery
The Loaves and Fishes Restaurant Recipe Book
The Sporting Cook Book

SECRETS OF COUNTRY COOKING

150 RECIPES FROM THE
LOAVES AND FISHES RESTAURANT

ANGELA F. RAWSON
AND
NIKKI ROWAN-KEDGE

Photographs by Amanda Heywood

Little, Brown and Company
BOSTON NEW YORK TORONTO LONDON

A LITTLE, BROWN BOOK

First published in the United Kingdom
by Little, Brown and Company (UK) in 1996

A CIP catalogue for this book is available
from the British Library

ISBN 0 316 87532 5

Typeset by Solidus (Bristol) Limited
Printed and bound in Great Britain by
Clays Ltd, St Ives plc

UK companies, institutions and other organisations wishing to make
bulk purchases of this or any other books published by Little, Brown,
should contact their local bookshop or the special sales department
at the address below.
Tel 0171 911 8000. Fax 0171 911 8100.

Little, Brown and Company (UK)
Brettenham House
Lancaster Place
London WC2E 7EN

Contents

Introduction

Cooking is therapeutic, and can have a calming influence on us and the people with whom we share the results of our labours. We all know the pleasure of eating a meal prepared with love. With this book we want to bring the joy back into cooking, using the best of British ingredients in traditional and modern country recipes.

Let us show our fellow Europeans that British food can, and does, hold its own alongside French, Italian, Swiss and German food. This is not to say that we cannot use ingredients from other countries to enhance our local cuisine, but if we support our enterprising organic farmers, traditional cheese-makers, fish- and meat-smokers, and all those free spirits who are keeping our real-food heritage alive by rearing animals compassionately and non-intensively, then we will be doing our bit to influence market forces, and once again we will be able to buy good, fresh, British food in the marketplace.

When Angela and I started out on our cookery adventure twenty-five years ago, we firmly believed that the foundation to this enterprise, as to any other, should be honesty. If we were true to ourselves, we would be true to others too.

This has been the basis of our food business through the years. We use nothing deep-frozen, nor any catering or microwave convenience food. All our ingredients are fresh, free-range, organically grown and non-intensively farmed. We buy local produce wherever possible. We give our business to farms that treat animals, and the land, well. We salute the French gourmet Curnonsky, who said, 'Cuisine is when things taste like themselves.'

The recipes in this book are designed to minimize the time spent in the kitchen, and they are not difficult to prepare. Angela's philosophy of cooking is to slow down, to treat each stage as complete in itself, to express love in your cooking, and to allow the process to bring you a feeling of fulfilment. We hope this book will play its part.

Nikki Rowan-Kedge

Notes on Measurements

Recipes give measurements in both metric and imperial units. For greatest accuracy, follow one system or the other, rather than alternating between both, for each recipe you use.

TABLESPOONS

The recipes use a 15ml tablespoon. All dry ingredients are measured in rounded tablespoons unless 'level' is stated. Two tablespoons of liquid ingredients correspond to 30ml/1fl oz.

TEASPOONS

Teaspoons hold 5ml and are always level.

CUP MEASURES

Some cooks, especially in the US, use volume (cup) rather than weight measures. The following weight-to-cup equivalents are designed to help these cooks. The cup used is an American one, which holds 8fl oz (16 × 15ml tablespoons/approximately 240ml).

Ingredient	Metric	Imperial	Volume
Butter	30g	1oz	2 tablespoons
	60g	2oz	4 tablespoons
	115g	4oz	½ cup
	230g	8oz	1 cup
Dried fruit	115g	4oz	½ cup
(unsoaked)	230g	8oz	1 cup
Flour	115g	4oz	1 cup
	170g	6oz	1½ cups
Rice (uncooked)	60g	2oz	¼ cup
	115g	4oz	½ cup
Sugar (white	115g	4oz	⅔ cup
and brown)	170g	6oz	1 cup
Sugar (icing/	140g	5oz	1 cup
confectioner's)			

Cooking Tips and Wrinkles

Our first tip: to keep the sparkle in champagne for a day or two, place a silver or silver-plated spoon in the bottle so that the bowl of the spoon is held by the bottle neck and return the bottle to the refrigerator. The spoon handle need not touch the champagne.

EGGS

Always use free-range eggs if you can get hold of them. Not only do free-range chickens have a better life, they also lay firmer, better-quality eggs than their stress-afflicted, battery-raised counterparts. If your mayonnaise does not set, for example, it may be that the eggs have been laid under stress and are thin and of poor quality.

Unless otherwise stated, the recipes here use size 3 (medium) eggs. Where large eggs are called for, use size 1. Size 2 are a compromise between 1 and 3, and size 4 are simply small.

Stored at room temperature, eggs will keep fresh for 9 to 10 days unless the weather is hot. In a cool larder they keep for around 12 days, and in the refrigerator for well over a month (after laying, not after purchase), though refrigerated eggs need 30 to 45 minutes to come around to room temperature before use.

To separate the yolk from the white, tap the egg smartly on the rim of a bowl to split the shell. Pass the yolk from one half of the shell to the other, allowing the whites to drip into the bowl. Have another bowl nearby into which to tip the yolk. Store separated eggs in the refrigerator in airtight containers. A layer of water or milk poured over yolks will prevent hardening. Yolks keep for 3 to 4 days, but whites only for 2 (a good excuse to make meringues).

CRUSHING GARLIC

For best results make garlic into a paste before cooking with it: crush the clove into a little salt, using the flat of a knife blade.

BREADCRUMBS

Take a few slices of stale white or wholemeal bread and gently dry out in a slow oven until crisp. Allow to cool, then whizz in a food processor until you have fine crumbs. If you do not have a food processor or blender, place the dried-out bread in a very strong plastic bag and crush it with a rolling pin. Store in an airtight container until required.

SHREDDING LEAVES

To shred leaves, such as lettuce, spinach, sorrel and cabbage, stack the washed leaves into small piles, roll into sausage shapes then slice through with a sharp knife.

PURÉEING WITHOUT A FOOD PROCESSOR OR BLENDER

Push solids through a sieve with a wooden spoon, or use a Mouli mill.

FREEZING/CHILLING

Encourage quicker freezing, if necessary, by inserting a metal spoon into an ice-cream or sorbet mixture: the metal conducts chilled air in. Remove the spoon before the mixture is frozen hard.

Chilling foods in individual portions also speeds up the process, as will using a metal container (which acts on the food in the same way as a metal spoon in an ice-cream mixture). However, food should not be left in a metal container once chilled: the metal can taint it.

OILS

The finest-flavoured oils are those made from the first pressing of nuts, seeds and olives. With the exception of sunflower oil these are not suitable for deep-frying, but make the best sauces and dressings. The best oils for frying are vegetable or sunflower oils.

Oils, especially the polyunsaturated varieties made from vegetable and sunflower oils, oxidize and turn rancid quickly and so are best stored in cool places away from direct sunlight. If oil is to be re-used after deep-frying, sieve out any impurities from the cooled oil before storing it. Oil used for frying should not be used more than 3 or 4 times.

Oil is an essential part of our diet, whether saturated (as animal fats are) or polyunsaturated, because it contains vitamin A and essential fatty acids. Vitamins and fancy names apart, good beef dripping is the best fat for deep-frying chips. A Lancastrian friend of ours always makes us chips fried in beef dripping – the best we have ever tasted. As with all things, when taken in moderation they do no harm, and when enjoyed they do a whole lot of good. We always make sure, however, that the animal-derived foods we use come from organically raised and properly looked after creatures.

DEEP-FRYING

A deep fat fryer or a deep pan with a wire basket is required for deep-frying. Use vegetable or sunflower oil that is clear and pure and free from moisture, and fill the container about three-quarters full. Allow the oil to reach the correct temperature before adding the food. If the oil is not hot enough, the food will be soggy and greasy; if too high, the food will burn. To test, drop a small piece of bread or raw potato into the oil. If it does not brown fairly quickly, heat the oil a little longer. If it burns almost at once, turn down the heat. If it quickly turns golden-brown, the oil is ready.

Deep-frying is used for croquettes, fritters, batter- or breadcrumb-coated food and, of course, chipped potatoes.

STEAMING

This is the gentle cooking of food in the vapour from liquid in a tightly closed pan. It preserves the flavour, colour and texture of food and retains a high level of minerals and vitamins. Only the freshest and best of ingredients should be steamed. The method is ideal for cooking fresh fish, shellfish and vegetables. Suet puddings, savoury and sweet, such as our Christmas pudding (page 174), are also cooked in a steamer. Dried fruit can be rehydrated by steaming over plain water for 4 to 5 minutes.

Purpose-made double saucepans with built-in steaming baskets are convenient to use. So too are Chinese bamboo baskets, placed on top of each other and allowing an entire meal to be cooked at the same time. You can also place an ordinary metal sieve or strainer with legs in a large pan. Providing the water does not touch the ingredients, this simple steamer works perfectly well.

Liquid for steaming can be plain water, water seasoned with herbs, salt and/or spices (for aromatic steaming), or beef, chicken or fish stock. The liquid must be of sufficient quantity not to boil or simmer away during cooking but must not touch the food. For vegetables such as spinach, use plain water. Steam fish either whole in its skin or in fillets rolled or placed lengthways in the basket. Fish, and in particular shellfish, can be steamed on a bed of fresh herbs or, if you can get it, edible seaweed.

PREPARING THE DISH FOR A CHILLED SOUFFLÉ

Cut a strip of greaseproof, parchment or wax paper, deep enough to reach from the base of the dish to 10cm/4 inches above its rim, and long enough to go around the dish with the ends overlapping by about 10cm/4 inches. Tie the paper around the outside with string and fasten securely so the string fits closely to the rim and prevents any mixture from escaping.

Pour the mixture into the dish to just above the rim, to give the appearance of the soufflé having risen. To release the soufflé, take a knife dipped into hot water and run it around the inside of the paper collar: the paper should then come away quite easily.

USING GELATINE

Powdered gelatine comes in small envelopes: 1 envelope sets 568ml/1 pint liquid. Dissolve the gelatine in a bowl of cold water, using the amount of water specified in the recipe. You may stand the bowl in a saucepan of hot water to encourage it to dissolve, but avoid overheating it because this interferes with its setting properties.

Leaf gelatine is finer, tasteless, and comes in thin sheets: 4 sheets set 568ml/1 pint liquid. It is slightly more tricky to use. Soak the sheets in cold water until they become floppy, then drop them into your hot sauce. If the sauce is cold, drop the sheets – after their cold-water soak – into the requisite amount of hot water (according to the recipe), then pour into the mixture.

Setting time depends on the coldness of your refrigerator. Once a good set has been reached, remove the dish from the refrigerator about 30 minutes before required to prevent the texture from becoming rubbery. If the dish is not setting quickly enough, put it into the freezer for 30 minutes, then return to the refrigerator.

Vegetarians may use arrowroot as an alternative setting agent. Follow the directions on the packet.

ASPIC

Aspic is a clear, savoury jelly, used in the moulding and presentation of cold foods. Use only top-quality aspic, which is quick dissolving and ready flavoured. Moisten with a little cold water, then dissolve in a little hot water or put directly into the hot sauce, as specified in the recipe. (Follow the recipe rather than the directions on the packet.)

You can make aspic at home but it is fairly time-consuming. Make a well-flavoured savoury meat or fish stock, using bones. Reduce well, allow to cool, then chill in the refrigerator. Skim any fat off the surface when cold and set. The gelatine in the bones should set the stock to a jelly; if it does not set firmly, add powdered or leaf gelatine (see above).

JARS FOR JAMS AND PRESERVES

Use jars and lids that have been thoroughly washed and then dried in the oven. Cut out a circle of greaseproof, parchment or wax paper, the diameter of the jar, and gently press it on top of the preserve before putting on the lid.

TESTING CAKES FOR DONENESS

In most cases the cake should feel firm to the touch in the centre when done. If you use a skewer to test the inside of the cake, warm the skewer first – a cold skewer may encourage the cake to sink. Leave a cake to relax in its tin for 10 minutes after removing from the oven. The cake shrinks a little when ready, and comes away more easily from the tin.

1
Soups

CHILLED CRAB SOUP

Our very first outside dinner party was at Charlton Park near Cirencester, the home of Lord and Lady Suffolk. We served chilled crab soup as a starter. Ten years on, after the magnificent manor house had been sold and split into luxury apartments, we were invited to a summer ball in honour of a friend's fortieth birthday. The ball was held in the hall and dining rooms of the house, the very rooms we had first ventured into when starting out in business. And on this occasion, already so nostalgic for us, we found ourselves eating chilled crab soup. The soup is now a long-established favourite, and as enjoyable now as it was when we first tried it.

SERVES 4 to 6

30g/1oz butter
1 onion, peeled and finely chopped
1 small bay leaf
1 small clove garlic, crushed with a little salt
1kg/2lb tomatoes, skinned (page 12) and deseeded
1 tablespoon tomato purée
1.4 litres/2½ pints chicken stock
3 teaspoons anchovy essence
1 dressed crab: brown and white meat
grated rind and juice of 1 small lemon
150ml/5fl oz double cream

Melt the butter in a saucepan, add the onion and cook until soft. Add the bay leaf, garlic and tomatoes, then cover, and cook until the tomatoes are soft and pulpy. Add the tomato purée, stock and anchovy essence, and simmer for 10 to 15 minutes.

Remove any pieces of shell from the crabmeat and put the brown meat into the soup mixture. Add the lemon rind and juice. Liquidize the soup until smooth, then transfer to a saucepan (it chills more quickly in a metal saucepan), or to a bowl if you prefer, stir in the cream and the white crabmeat, and chill until required.

CHILLED SMOKED SALMON SOUP

A lovely soup for a summer lunch or dinner party, and a change from smoked salmon with a wedge of lemon. It is easy to prepare and can be left to chill to await your pleasure. If raw spring onion is not to your taste, put it into a little oil and sauté for a couple of minutes, then use as described in the recipe.

SERVES 4 to 6

4 spring onions, white part only, chopped
300ml/10fl oz tomato juice
a few shakes of Tabasco
3 teaspoons tomato purée
juice of 1 lemon
250g/8oz smoked salmon trimmings
3 tablespoons mayonnaise
600ml/1 pint fish stock
salt and freshly ground black pepper
150ml/5fl oz fromage frais or single cream
125g/4oz peeled prawns
4 to 6 quail eggs, hard-boiled and cut in half
4 sprigs fresh fennel

Liquidize the spring onion, tomato juice, Tabasco to taste, tomato purée and lemon juice until smooth. Add the smoked salmon and liquidize again until smooth. Pour the soup into a large bowl and whisk in the mayonnaise, stock, seasonings and fromage frais or cream. Pour into chilled soup bowls, and place in the refrigerator to chill. When chilled, divide the prawns equally among the soup bowls, float 2 halves of quail eggs on top of each one and place a sprig of fennel over the egg. Serve with brown bread and butter.

CHILLED CURRIED MANGO SOUP

This is a delightful summer soup, ideal for *al fresco* meals whether in the garden or on a picnic. It is also a wonderful starter to serve when entertaining because you can prepare it in advance, you do not have to keep it warm, and it is ready and waiting while you sip your aperitif with your guests. If you also choose other courses that are prepared ahead, then you can feel like a guest at your own party, which is just how it should be. Fresh mangoes with a strong perfume are essential for a good-flavoured soup. With apple juice as the stock, the soup is suitable for vegetarians.

SERVES 4 to 6

120ml/4fl oz vegetable oil
2 medium onions, peeled and finely chopped
4 eating apples, peeled, cored and chopped
850ml/1½ pints apple juice
3 ripe mangoes, skinned, stoned and chopped
juice of 2 lemons
2 to 3 teaspoons curry paste
3 teaspoons mango chutney
salt and freshly ground white pepper
180ml/6fl oz Greek yoghurt or single cream

Put the oil into a saucepan, add the onion and apple and cook gently until soft but not brown. Pour in the apple juice and simmer for 10 minutes.

Remove from the heat and add the mango, lemon juice, curry paste, mango chutney and seasonings. Liquidize the soup a little at a time until smooth and creamy, then pour into a saucepan (it chills more quickly in a metal saucepan), or into a bowl if you prefer. Whisk in the yoghurt or cream, then chill until required.

LEEK AND LOVAGE SOUP

Lovage is an aromatic herb that used to proliferate in old herb gardens. Years ago country inns would serve lovage as a cordial, or mixed with brandy as a remedy for an upset stomach, but we have found that not many people know about this lovely English herb these days. If you are able to get a root, even a small one, it will grow very easily in the garden and will multiply itself greatly. The leaves have the flavour of curried celery, and the herb is one of our very favourite ones. Our plant grows to about 3 feet in the summer and if, when mowing the grass, some of the lower leaves are accidentally mown over, the smell is enough to send the tastebuds jumping and demanding to be plied with this wonderful herb. The young shredded leaves are delicious in a salad, and the aromatic flavour also gives a piquancy to soups, mousses and stews.

SERVES 4 to 6

60g/2oz unsalted butter
3 medium leeks, split down the centre, cleaned and chopped
750g/1¼lb potatoes, peeled and thinly sliced
300ml/10fl oz milk
600ml/1 pint chicken or vegetable stock
salt and freshly ground white pepper
20 or so leaves fresh lovage
4 sprigs fresh parsley
a little single cream to garnish (optional)

Melt the butter in a saucepan, add the leeks and potatoes and cook gently until soft but not brown. Pour in the milk and stock, season to taste and cook over a very low heat for about 15 to 20 minutes.

Snip the herbs into the soup, then liquidize until smooth. Pour the soup back into a clean saucepan to reheat it, and swirl in the cream, if using.

LETTUCE AND ASPARAGUS SOUP

A fresh lettuce can be a rarity in some of the larger supermarkets and greengrocers but we are lucky enough to get ours from the gardens at Chilton Manor, lovingly tended by the head gardener, Harry Dodson. The lettuce is crisp, green and full of crunchy flavour. We once kept a couple of Harry's lettuces for a week, and they were as crisp then as on the day they were first cut – a sign of a true fresh lettuce. This is a summer soup for a chilly summer's evening and it looks extremely attractive garnished with steamed asparagus tips and a swirl of cream. If you have time, pipe a rosette of cream on the soup instead of a swirl. A rosette floats on top of the soup for longer.

SERVES 4 to 6

125g/4oz lettuce
250g/8oz fresh asparagus
60g/2oz butter
1 large onion, peeled and chopped
½ clove garlic, crushed with a little salt
300ml/10fl oz vegetable or chicken stock
salt and freshly ground black pepper
freshly grated nutmeg
small bunch fresh tarragon leaves, finely chopped
450ml/15fl oz milk
120ml/4fl oz single cream

Wash the lettuce and cut into small strips. Trim any woody parts from the base of the asparagus and discard. Cut off the tips of the asparagus, reserve for garnishing the soup, and chop the remaining asparagus stems into small pieces.

Melt the butter in a large saucepan and add the onion. Cook until just softening but not brown. Stir in the garlic, then add the strips of lettuce and stir until heated through. Add the chopped asparagus, pour in the stock, add seasonings and nutmeg to taste and bring to simmering point. Cook gently until the asparagus has softened.

Liquidize the soup until smooth and return to a clean saucepan. If the asparagus is still a little stringy, strain the soup through a sieve first.

Stir in the tarragon, milk and cream and check the seasonings. Cut the asparagus tips in half lengthways and steam for a couple of minutes. Reheat the soup but do not boil. Serve hot, garnished with the asparagus tips and a rosette or swirl of cream.

CREAM OF CARROT AND CORIANDER SOUP

Mrs Beeton in her book of *Household Management* tells us that garden carrots were first introduced to Britain during the reign of Elizabeth I. They were so highly esteemed that fashionable ladies wore the leaves in their head-dresses. Fashion apart, the carrot is a much used and very versatile vegetable for soups and stews. When not using our own home-grown carrots, we prefer to buy organically grown ones. Occasionally necessity has forced us to buy packaged carrots, and we have noticed that after a couple of days they start to turn black – some sort of chemical reaction to overfertilization? – whereas home-grown or organically grown carrots keep well for a couple of weeks. This soup is nutritious and quick to make. It can be served just as it is, or with fried bread croûtons. If vegetable stock is used instead of chicken stock, it is suitable for vegetarians. It freezes well after liquidizing, but do not add the cream until the soup is required.

SERVES 4

30g / 1oz unsalted butter
90ml / 3fl oz vegetable oil
500g / 1lb carrots, peeled and thinly sliced
1 large onion, peeled and finely chopped
1 small clove garlic, crushed with a little salt
850ml / 1½ pints vegetable or chicken stock
10 coriander seeds
1 small bay leaf
salt and freshly ground black pepper
90ml / 3fl oz double cream

Melt the butter with the oil in a large saucepan. Add the carrot, onion and garlic, cover, and sweat the vegetables for a couple of minutes until soft. Then pour in the stock, add the coriander seeds, bay leaf and seasonings, and simmer for 25 minutes.

Remove the bay leaf and liquidize the soup, then add the cream. Check the seasonings and reheat the soup if necessary but do not allow it to boil once the cream has been added.

CAULIFLOWER AND MINT SOUP

Fresh cauliflower is a must for this recipe. We have in the past been given soup made from leftover cooked cauliflower, grey in colour and smelling like boiled dishcloths. Made with a good firm fresh cauliflower, this soup is delightful. Do include the tender stalk, which has lots of flavour. Take care not to overcook the cauliflower, and be sure to enjoy this fresh-tasting soup as soon as it is made because it will not keep for long.

SERVES 4

90g/3oz unsalted butter
2 large onions, peeled and chopped
1 small clove garlic, crushed with a little salt
1 small fresh English cauliflower, cut into even-sized pieces, small green
leaves reserved for garnish
850ml/1½ pints vegetable or chicken stock
salt and freshly ground black pepper
150ml/5fl oz single cream
3 tablespoons finely chopped fresh mint
a little milk to slacken the soup (optional)

Melt the butter in a fairly large saucepan and put in the onion and garlic. Stir for a couple of minutes then add the cauliflower pieces. Stir together for another minute or so then pour in the stock. Season to taste and simmer until the cauliflower is cooked but still firm. Allow the cooked soup to cool a little, then liquidize until smooth. Return the soup to a clean saucepan, add most of the cream and mint (reserve the remainder to garnish the soup), check the seasonings and reheat. Do not boil. Should the soup be too thick, pour in a little milk to slacken it until it reaches the required consistency. Serve at once with a small cauliflower leaf in the centre and a little mint sprinkled over. Put a swirl of cream on top if desired.

CELERIAC AND ALMOND SOUP

Celeriac, as its name implies, has the flavour of strong celery. It is a much underrated vegetable, and this is a simple but fine way to serve it. Try to buy the smoothest celeriac you can. The more knobbly the celeriac the harder to peel and the more waste there will be. For most uses the peeled celeriac should be soaked in vinegar mixed with water, or rubbed over with lemon, to avoid discolouration, but there's no need to do this when you are making soup.

SERVES 4 to 6

60g/2oz butter
1 large, smooth as possible celeriac, peeled and finely chopped
1 large onion or 3 large shallots, peeled and chopped
850ml/1½ pints chicken stock
salt and freshly ground black pepper
90ml/3fl oz double cream
2 tablespoons slivered almonds, lightly toasted

Melt the butter in a large saucepan, add the celeriac and onion or shallots, cover, and cook until the celeriac is tender. Pour in the stock, season to taste and cook for a further 15 minutes.

Allow the soup to cool a little, then liquidize until smooth. Return the soup to a clean saucepan, stir in the cream and check the seasonings. Serve hot with the toasted almonds scattered over the top.

TOMATO, RED PEPPER
AND BASIL SOUP

Whenever Angela's mother entertains, she telephones Angela to check that she has made a dish correctly, or to ask what she should do if something has not turned out well. This makes entertaining costly since Madame Rawson lives in France. Recipes such as this one should cut the phone bills – they have been chosen for simplicity of instruction and ease of preparation as well as wonderful taste. And if we have not succeeded in this, Angela's mother will certainly telephone and say so. To skin tomatoes: place them in a large basin and cover with boiling water. Allow to stand in the water for a couple of minutes, then with a slotted spoon remove from the hot water and place in a bowl of cold water. The skin should rub or peel away quite easily. If it does not, put the tomatoes back into boiling water and repeat the process until the skin does come away. If the skin is very difficult to remove, the tomato is not ripe.

SERVES 4 to 6

180ml/6fl oz olive oil
2 large onions, peeled and chopped
2 red peppers, cored, deseeded and chopped
1kg/2lb well-ripened, good-flavoured tomatoes, skinned, deseeded and
hard cores removed
1 clove garlic, crushed with a little salt
600ml/1 pint chicken stock
300ml/10fl oz tomato juice
1 level tablespoon sugar
4 teaspoons tomato purée
2 teaspoons sundried tomato paste
salt and freshly ground black pepper
1 bay leaf
chopped fresh basil leaves

Heat the oil in a saucepan and add the onion. Cook until just soft, then add the peppers, stir well and cook for a further few minutes. Chop the tomatoes and add to the pan together with the garlic, stock, tomato juice, sugar, tomato purée, sundried tomato paste, seasonings and bay leaf. Simmer for 20 minutes.

Remove from the heat, discard the bay leaf and allow the soup to cool a little. Liquidize in small quantities until smooth, then reheat. Stir in most of the basil, and serve with the remaining basil sprinkled over.

BUTTER BEAN AND BACON SOUP

It was early March and we were hard at work on this cookery book. Outside it was blowing, sleeting and snowing all at the same time, and, as usual when I am typing out recipes, I got very hungry. The next day was market day, our main shopping day, and the larder was almost empty. In the store cupboard (where we keep an emergency supply of iron rations, a preoccupation of mine ever since I read Enid Blyton's *Five on an Island* back in my schooldays) we found a tin of butter beans. So Angela gathered up the soup ingredients that we always have in stock: bacon, onion, garlic, oil and some herbs, and 25 minutes later a new soup was born that is delicious as well as warming and slightly unusual. This is a soup for emergencies or when battened down at home due to inclement weather.

SERVES 4

180ml / 6fl oz vegetable oil
4 rashers streaky bacon, rind removed
1 large onion, peeled and finely chopped
2 sticks celery, finely chopped
1 small clove garlic, crushed with a little salt
1 large tin (430g / 14oz) or 2 small tins (200g / 7oz) butter beans,
drained
1 teaspoon coriander seeds, crushed
salt and freshly ground black pepper
700ml / 1¼ pints chicken stock
120ml / 4fl oz double or single cream
chopped fresh parsley to garnish

Warm the oil in a large saucepan. Chop the bacon into small pieces and fry until brown and crispy. Remove from the pan with a slotted spoon and set aside. Add the onion and celery to the pan, stir well, cover, and cook gently until soft. Then add the garlic, stir well, and cook for a further couple of minutes. Add the butter beans, along with their liquid, to the pan, together with the coriander seeds and seasonings. Pour in the stock and simmer for about 20 minutes.

Remove the soup from the heat and liquidize until smooth. Return to a clean saucepan, put in the bacon and cream, stir and heat through without boiling. Serve hot with parsley sprinkled over the top.

CHILLI BEAN SOUP

This recipe came about one evening as we were eating chilli con carne. I happened to remark that the mixture would make a great winter soup, and the very next day Angela began experimenting. Soon this chilli bean soup evolved, which appears regularly on our restaurant menu during the colder months of the year and is truly satisfying.

SERVES 4 to 6

60ml/2fl oz vegetable oil
2 onions, peeled and finely chopped
1 clove garlic, crushed with a little salt
125g/4oz minced beef
1 tin (200g/7oz) chopped tomatoes, with their juice
1 tin (200g/7oz) red kidney beans, with their liquid
600ml/1 pint chicken stock
1 level tablespoon tomato purée
1 tablespoon demerara sugar
1 teaspoon chilli powder
300ml/10fl oz tomato juice
salt and freshly ground black pepper
a little extra water to slacken the soup (optional)
a little freshly grated Parmesan cheese to serve (please, not from a tub)

Put the oil into a saucepan, add the onion and cook until soft and golden. Add the garlic and beef and cook for 10 minutes. Pour in the tomatoes and kidney beans with their liquids and the stock, then add the tomato purée, sugar, chilli powder, tomato juice and seasonings. Bring up to simmering point and continue simmering for 1 hour, stirring from time to time. Should the soup reduce and become too thick, add a little extra water until you have the required consistency. Cook a little longer if you do add extra water; the extra cooking will improve the flavour. Serve hot with freshly grated Parmesan cheese scattered over the top.

MUSHROOM AND GINGER SOUP

According to the great cookery writer Mrs Beeton, 'Ginger is generally considered to be less pungent and heating to the system than might be expected from its effects on the organs of taste; it is frequently used, with considerable effect, as an anti-spasmodic and carminative.' Fortunately we have not had the first-hand experience of colic or gripe with which to verify Mrs Beeton's remarks. We do know, however, that adding ginger turns a fairly ordinary soup into one that is just a little different, and gives it a 'bite'. This soup is also easy and quick to prepare, and freezes well.

SERVES 4 to 6

125g/4oz unsalted butter
2 large onions, peeled and chopped
1 clove garlic, crushed with a little salt
2.5cm/1-inch piece of fresh root ginger, peeled and finely grated
250g/8oz mushrooms, washed and sliced
3 pieces of preserved ginger, chopped
850ml/1½ pints chicken or meat stock
salt and freshly ground black pepper
4 teaspoons cornflour, mixed with 120ml/4fl oz water (optional)
chopped fresh parsley to garnish

Melt the butter in a large saucepan. Add the onion, garlic and root ginger and cook until the onion becomes golden and is slightly caramelized. Then stir in the mushrooms and preserved ginger, and pour in the stock. Season well and simmer for about 45 minutes. For a thicker soup, add the slackened cornflour and blend in well. Serve hot with parsley sprinkled over.

ROASTED GARLIC AND MARROW SOUP

In the early days of our outside catering company we were asked to provide a lunch for fourteen vintage-car enthusiasts on their return to the house after a car rally. The gardener was to let us in so we could get the food prepared and the tables set. We arrived about 10.30 a.m. but there was no sign of the gardener. After an hour, and still no gardener, we looked around the house for a way in. At the back we found two large French windows with the shutters pulled to and only loosely secured. I discovered that I could open one just enough to squeeze through into the study. I found my way to the front door and opened it to a very relieved Angela. At that moment all the alarm bells began to ring. Angela told me to shut the doors to block out the sound so she could get on with the cooking (she is always calm in a crisis), and after about 10 minutes the house was surrounded by police, accompanied, to our relief, by the missing gardener, who had forgotten all about us until he heard the alarm. Eventually we were left to get on with our cooking, but with all the distractions, and this being only our second or third party, Angela made enough soup to feed an army. The vintage-car enthusiasts had to eat this soup for days afterwards. Fortunately, they liked it. Garlic becomes mild with roasting, but if you really do not like a lot, use less than in the recipe here.

SERVES 6

1 whole head of garlic
180ml / 6fl oz olive oil
60g / 2oz butter
1 medium onion, peeled and finely chopped
1 small marrow, peeled, cut in half and seeds removed
850ml / 1 1/2 pints chicken or vegetable stock
salt and freshly ground white pepper
150ml / 5fl oz single cream
small bunch fresh chives, finely snipped with scissors

Preheat the oven to 200°C/400°F/gas 6.

Break the garlic into individual cloves, removing the centre stalk and root end. Do not remove the papery skin. Put into a roasting tin and spoon the olive oil over, tossing the cloves about until well covered. Roast in the preheated oven for 15 to 20 minutes until soft and brown. Poke with the point of a knife to test for softness. When ready, remove from the oven and allow to cool enough to handle. Then, with the back of a knife, press the garlic out of its skin. Discard the skin and put the pulp to one side.

Melt the butter in a large saucepan, add the onion and cook until soft. Cut the marrow into cubes and add to the onion in the saucepan. Pour in the stock, add the garlic, season well and cover. Cook gently until the marrow is soft. Remove the pan from the heat, allow to cool a little, then liquidize until smooth. Stir in the cream and chopped chives and heat through when required but do not boil.

MURPHY SPECIAL
(A POTATO AND ONION SOUP)

One cold, blowy, wet November evening we had friends to dinner and, soup being a great favourite of theirs, invented this recipe in their honour. In Ireland a potato is traditionally called a murphy, and this was also the surname of our guests. On winter evenings this soup is deliciously warming and comforting, and it is also economical and easy to make. It is best served in earthenware bowls, accompanied by thick hunks of homemade bread spread with real English butter, and eaten sitting by a roaring fire. Use vegetable stock instead of chicken for a vegetarian version.

SERVES 6 to 8

60g/2oz butter
2 medium onions, peeled and finely chopped
3 medium floury potatoes (such as Desirée), peeled and
cut into small cubes
handful spring onion tops, finely chopped
good handful fresh chives, snipped with scissors
1.1 litres/2 pints good vegetable or chicken stock
salt and freshly ground black pepper
pinch of freshly grated nutmeg
20 or so leaves fresh mint, finely cut
120ml/4fl oz double or single cream (optional)

Melt the butter in a saucepan, add the onion and potatoes, cover and sauté, stirring occasionally. When the onion has softened, put in the spring onions and chives, replace the lid and cook for a further few minutes. Pour in the stock, season well and add the nutmeg. Simmer over a low heat until the potato is just beginning to thicken the soup but still retains some of its shape.

Stir in the mint and the cream, if using. Keep warm until required.

2

Light Dishes

ASPARAGUS MOUSSE

Tender asparagus is a must for this recipe. Choose crisp, firm spears, with the root end clean and white, and use as soon as possible. Asparagus with a yellow tinge at the root end is old and may be woody. Fresh asparagus tastes wonderful, and is also rich in fibre, low in calories, and contains vitamins A, B and C. This is a delicately flavoured mousse: none of the ingredients must overpower the asparagus or you will get a garlic or tarragon mousse instead. The salt is important in bringing out the flavour, but be careful not to overdo it. Serve with a green salad tossed in a light hazelnut oil dressing.

SERVES 6

450ml/15fl oz water
500g/1lb asparagus, trimmed
15g/½oz gelatine, softened in 150ml/5fl oz cold water
1 small clove garlic, crushed with a little salt
125g/4oz cream cheese
2 sprigs fresh tarragon, finely snipped with scissors
salt

Bring the water to the boil in a saucepan. Put the asparagus into the boiling water and cook quickly until the root end is tender. Remove and drain, reserving 300ml/10fl oz of the water. Pour the reserved asparagus water into the softened gelatine and blend well.

Trim away the asparagus tips (about 2.5cm/1 inch in length) and reserve for garnish. Liquidize the remaining asparagus with the dissolved gelatine in a blender until the mixture is smooth. Pour half the purée into a bowl, and to the half remaining in the blender add the garlic, cream cheese and tarragon. Blend until completely smooth, then add to the asparagus purée in the bowl and mix well. Season with a little salt. When thoroughly amalgamated, pour the mixture into 6 deep ramekins and chill in the refrigerator until set (at least 1½ hours in ceramic ramekins; less in metal ones).

When required, dip the ramekins quickly into boiling water to loosen the sides. Turn the mousses out on to plates, garnish with the asparagus tips and serve.

ASPARAGUS FLORENTINE

This is a variation on the classic Eggs Florentine. One evening in the restaurant we had a number of vegetarian guests, a lot of fresh spinach and a few bunches of English asparagus, and so, as necessity encourages creativity, a new vegetarian dish was born. It proved so popular that non-vegetarians ordered it too. Serve as a first course or a main dish.

SERVES 8 AS A STARTER, 4 AS A MAIN COURSE

500g / 1lb fresh spinach, washed and tough stalks removed
salt and freshly ground black pepper to taste
a little butter
16 spears fresh asparagus
1 recipe quantity Cheshire cheese sauce (page 242)
or onion sauce (page 243)

Cook the spinach in a steamer or in very little water until just soft: it needs to be cooked but still retain its crispness. Drain very thoroughly, season to taste and add a little butter. Mix together well and break up any leaves that are too large.

Steam the asparagus for a few minutes. Divide the spinach evenly between 4 warmed dinner plates, then place 4 asparagus spears on top of each pile of spinach. Dot with a little more butter, sprinkle with a little more salt and pepper and serve with the cheese or onion sauce.

STILTON AND SPRING ONION MOUSSE

Stilton appears quite often in our recipes one way or another: it's versatile, full of flavour and almost always in our larder. You can, of course, use any other blue cheese, as long as it has a good strong flavour but is not over-ripe (or the taste will be bitter). Then again, all those who are opposed to Stilton will tell you that *Stilton* is bitter – which of course it is not when properly matured and kept. Angela has to make this mousse in large quantities because it is so good that it disappears before you can say 'spring onion'. Turned out on to a china serving dish and decorated with cucumber butterflies, spring onion flowers and a small, fresh, appropriately coloured edible flower, this mousse looks stunning on a buffet table. Make sure your guests see it before the knife or spoon is plunged in. To make spring onion flowers, trim the root end of the spring onion well. Peel off the transparent skin. With a sharp knife, make 4 cuts through the white part of the onion (so that you cut it into eighths), leaving the green part whole, then place in iced water until the ends curl. To make cucumber butterflies, simply make 2 cuts in a thin slice of cucumber, leaving the centre intact. Then twist the slice.

SERVES 6

30g/1oz unsalted butter
4 spring onions, thinly sliced
30g/1oz plain flour
300ml/10fl oz milk
175g/6oz Stilton cheese
2 free-range eggs, separated
freshly ground black pepper
24g/just under 1oz aspic, dissolved in 240ml/8fl oz water
120ml/4fl oz double cream
slices of cucumber, spring onions, edible flowers to garnish

Melt the butter in a saucepan, add the spring onions and cook for a few minutes. Remove the onions from the pan and set aside. Add the flour to the pan and cook for a few minutes until you have a roux. Pour in the milk and blend together until you have a thick white sauce. Remove the pan from the heat and crumble in the cheese.

Add the egg yolks to the white sauce. Season to taste with black pepper, then pour in the dissolved aspic. Transfer to a food-processor bowl and liquidize.

Whip the cream until it just holds its shape. In a separate bowl beat the egg whites until stiff. Allow the liquidized sauce to cool a little, then transfer to a new bowl for chilling if necessary, and fold in the cream. Season with black pepper. Fold in the spring onions and, finally, the beaten egg white. Chill in the refrigerator for at least a couple of hours until set.

Dip quickly into boiling water to loosen the sides, turn out on to a serving dish and garnish before serving.

CHILLED HAM MOUSSE

A great favourite with us and with our friends for a buffet, lunch or dinner party, whatever the season. It is a meal in itself, and can also accompany a variety of salads with rice or potatoes. If you feel inclined, make a homemade mayonnaise flavoured with fresh tarragon to accompany the mousse or to mix into cold, chopped potatoes for a salad to serve alongside. The mousse can be made in individual moulds and turned out on to small plates, or it can be made in one large bowl and spooned out as required, like a soufflé. If you are going to spoon it out, you need not set the garnish in aspic in the dish, as described at the start of the recipe. Instead, garnish the mousse with the lemon rind and cucumber strips on serving. The basis of the recipe is béchamel sauce, a 'foundation' sauce important for many recipes. You can make a chilled chicken mousse too, using cooked and minced chicken leftovers instead of the ham.

SERVES 6

24g/just under 1oz aspic, dissolved in 300ml/10fl oz water
slices of cucumber, strips of lemon rind, a few leaves
of tarragon to garnish
350g/12oz minced cooked ham (or chicken)
150ml/5fl oz béchamel sauce (page 240)
1 teaspoon finely chopped fresh French tarragon
salt and freshly ground black pepper
3 tablespoons mayonnaise
150ml/5fl oz whipping cream, lightly whipped

Line a large bowl or soufflé dish or 6 individual ramekins with a little of the dissolved aspic jelly (unless you plan to spoon out the soufflé; see the introduction above) and allow to set. Once set, decorate the bottom of the bowl or ramekins with the cucumber slices, lemon rind and tarragon leaves.

Mix together the minced ham or chicken, béchamel sauce and tarragon and season to taste. Pour in the remaining aspic. When the mixture is on the point of setting, fold in the mayonnaise and whipped cream. Transfer to the serving dish(es) and return to the refrigerator to set completely (1 to 2 hours for individual mousses, up to 6 hours for one large one).

When the mousse has set, dip the bowl or ramekins quickly into boiling water to loosen the sides and turn out on to a serving dish. Garnish with a little extra lemon rind and cucumber if desired.

GREEN VEGETABLE TERRINE

It was my forty-second birthday, and Angela had prepared a surprise picnic brunch. I was bundled, blindfolded, into the car and taken along a bumpy track for what seemed like miles. On arrival I was led out and allowed to remove the blindfold. In front of me in an old hay barn was a small group of friends, a bottle of Krug champagne and a basket full of food which included, among other things, this vegetable terrine. Transported in its loaf tin, then cut into slices, it is an ideal dish for picnics or summer buffets in or out of the garden. The weather was glorious, as it usually is on my birthday – if you are planning a picnic or an *al fresco* meal, 16 June is a very good bet for fine weather.

SERVES 4 to 6

½ small cucumber, peeled and diced
2 teaspoons salt
125g/4oz fresh asparagus, trimmed and washed
90g/3oz shelled fresh peas
10 large fresh spinach leaves, large stalks removed
small bunch fresh tarragon, chopped
small bunch fresh chives, snipped with scissors
freshly ground black pepper
500g/1lb curd cheese or cottage cheese, mashed
90ml/3fl oz tarragon vinegar
24g/just under 1oz aspic, dissolved in 240ml/8fl oz water
150ml/5fl oz single cream
2 spring onions, white parts only, thinly sliced

Put the cucumber into a colander, sprinkle with the salt and stir to cover the cucumber well. Press down on the cucumber with a plate and leave to drain for 20 minutes.

Meanwhile, steam the asparagus until just tender. For the last couple of minutes of steaming time, add the peas and lightly steam them too. Remove the asparagus and peas from the steamer and set aside to cool.

Quickly steam the spinach leaves (for about 3 seconds). Remove and rinse under cold running water and drain well. Allow to cool, then use to line a 250g/8oz loaf tin.

Put the herbs, pepper, cheese and vinegar into a bowl and beat together. Gradually pour in the dissolved aspic, beating well as you go. Then add the cream and stir until well blended.

Press the plate down hard on to the cucumber to remove any excess liquid, then fold the cucumber into the cheese and cream mixture. Fold in the spring onion, then pour half the mixture into the prepared loaf tin. Allow to set slightly (an hour or so in the refrigerator), then lay the asparagus and peas over it, reserving a few asparagus spears for decoration. Pour the remaining half of the cheese mixture into the tin, and put in the refrigerator to set fully (several hours or overnight). When set, dip quickly into boiling water to loosen the sides, turn out on to a serving dish and decorate with the reserved asparagus. Use a sharp knife to slice the terrine cleanly.

CHICKEN LIVER AND ORANGE TERRINE

When I was small the very sight of liver or any offal would have me pretending to be at some urgent business in my room. I was forever being forced out of hiding and made to eat a dry, leathery offering, the taste somewhere between burnt cardboard and old wool. I have now conquered my aversion to liver. When it is cooked properly and served with a suitable sauce, it is nutritious and heavenly food. This terrine is easy to make, and ideal for a dinner party because it should be prepared a day in advance and allowed to set and chill. Serve with hot buttered toast or French bread and a fresh green salad for a first course or a light lunch. Excellent for picnics.

SERVES 4 to 6

60g/2oz unsalted butter
1 small onion, peeled and finely chopped
1 small clove garlic, crushed with a little salt
4 rashers streaky bacon, rind removed, cut into small pieces
1 bay leaf
grated rind of ½ orange
1 teaspoon chopped fresh thyme
250g/8oz chicken livers, trimmed and cut into small pieces
salt and freshly ground black pepper

Melt the butter in a frying pan and add the onion and garlic. As soon as the onion begins to soften, add the bacon. Cook until the bacon fat begins to run, then add the bay leaf, orange rind and thyme. Stir well, then add the chicken liver and cook for 5 to 7 minutes. Season to taste. Put the mixture into a food processor or blender and blend until smooth. Pour into individual ramekins or one terrine dish and chill overnight.

BLUE CHEESE TARTLETS

'Many a one has been comforted in their sorrow by seeing a good dish come upon the table,' says Mrs Gaskell in *Cranford*. These cheese tartlets are certainly a good dish to have on the table as a first course, or to serve as a savoury alternative to a pudding, and you do not have to be sorrowful to enjoy them. We often have these tartlets for lunch, when Angela makes a fresh green salad over which she crumbles extra blue cheese and, her favourite thing, walnuts. As a main course, allow two (or more) tartlets per person.

MAKES 8 × 6 CM / 2½ INCH TARTLETS

250g / 8oz wholemeal shortcrust pastry (page 234)

FOR THE FILLING:
150ml / 5fl oz béchamel sauce (page 240)
150ml / 5fl oz double cream
3 free-range egg yolks
125g / 4oz blue cheese

Preheat the oven to 190°C/375°F/gas 5.

Roll out the pastry, cut out 8 circles and line the 6cm/2½-inch tartlet tins with them. Cut out a lid for each tartlet from the remaining pastry.

In a food processor or blender, combine all the filling ingredients together until smooth. (If you do not have a food processor or blender, cream the cheese with a little milk, then blend all the ingredients together well with a fork.) Fill each pastry case about three-quarters full. Rest a pastry lid on top of each one without pressing down hard. Bake in the preheated oven for about 20 minutes or until golden-brown. Serve hot, straight from the oven.

JELLIED TOMATO AND BASIL CONSOMMÉ

Looking through a pile of old cookbooks, we came across a version of this recipe. It gave us an idea for what to do with several pounds of tomatoes we had been given by a neighbour. Tested and adapted, a fairly ordinary 'tomato mould' (its original name) became transformed into a lovely, refreshing and slightly unusual starter. The centre of the ring can be filled with a variety of ingredients, such as fresh basil, prawns in a mayonnaise sauce, chopped cucumber, peas and chopped spring onion, cooked rice with or without chopped hard-boiled egg, smoked salmon, trout. We had great fun experimenting with various combinations, the most outrageous of which often turned out to be the best. However, it is wise, if you are not sure whether the ingredients will work, to make a small quantity and to test it rather than piling it all into the ring and then finding it unpalatable.

SERVES 8 to 10

1kg/2lb ripe tomatoes, skinned (page 12) and chopped
2 bay leaves
300ml/10fl oz dry white wine
4 tablespoons white wine vinegar
1 level tablespoon tomato purée
1 clove garlic, crushed with a little salt
grated rind and juice of 1 lemon
1 tablespoon demerara sugar
salt and freshly ground white pepper
24g/just under 1oz aspic, dissolved in 150ml/5fl oz water
a few cherry tomatoes (optional)
6 large leaves fresh basil

Put the tomatoes, bay leaves, wine, wine vinegar, tomato purée, garlic, lemon rind and juice, sugar, salt and pepper into a large pan. Take care over the salt: not too much as you already have some mixed in with the garlic. Simmer for 10 to 15 minutes until the sugar has dissolved. Turn off the heat and allow all the ingredients to infuse for 20 minutes.

Pour the dissolved aspic into the pan and stir well in. Taste and check the seasonings. Strain through a fine sieve into a large bowl. Lightly oil a ring mould and pour in the strained tomato mixture. If desired, dot cherry tomatoes around so that they set into the mould. Chop the basil and sprinkle it over the tomato mixture.

Allow the tomato mould to set in the refrigerator (at least 4 hours, or overnight). Before serving, turn the mould out on to a dish and pile your chosen filling into the centre.

STILTON AND PEAR FLANS

One evening, at our previous restaurant in the Marlborough Downs hamlet of Rockley, the late Jane Grigson and her husband Geoffrey came to dinner. All went well until the cheese course, when I presented our truckle of Stilton cheese wrapped in a white damask napkin. Resting on top of this wonderful cheese was a Victorian silver and bone-handled Stilton scoop. We were very pleased with this acquisition, which we had found in an antique shop some years before. Not so Jane Grigson. She was of the school of thought that cutting a wedge of Stilton with a knife was the correct method and on no account should a scoop or spoon be used. (Why then did the Victorians make hundreds of Stilton scoops?) Now I place the scoop and a knife on top of the cheese so guests can do as they choose. Serve any leftover Stilton as a soup or a mousse, or as here in a flan with fresh pears – a wonderful combination. Other blue cheeses can be substituted but our favourite is a good-flavoured and well-matured Stilton. This savoury flan is ideal for lunch or supper. Accompany with a fresh green salad scattered with chopped hazelnuts or almonds, small pieces of pear, even a little more crumbled Stilton. Pour a little walnut oil over the salad and season with freshly ground black pepper.

MAKES 6 × 10–12 CM/4–5 INCH FLANS

350g/12oz wholemeal shortcrust pastry (page 234)
30g/1oz chopped walnuts
60g/2oz peeled and diced ripe pear (about half a large pear; reserve the remainder for a salad)
125g/4oz mature blue Stilton cheese, crumbled
a few sprigs fresh thyme
2 free-range eggs
salt and freshly ground black pepper
150ml/5fl oz single cream plus 4 tablespoons milk
a few sprigs fresh parsley to garnish

Preheat the oven to 200°C/400°F/gas 6.

Line 6 small (10–12cm/4–5-inch) flan tins with the shortcrust pastry and bake blind in the preheated oven for 20 to 25 minutes, removing the lining paper and baking beans halfway through. During the last 10 minutes of cooking time, on the shelf below the flans, toast the walnut pieces on a baking tray. Remove the flan cases and walnuts, and turn the oven down to 190°C/375°F/gas 5.

Divide the walnuts, pear and cheese between the baked flan cases. Strip the leaves from the thyme, discarding the woody stems, and strew the leaves generously over the pear and cheese mixture.

Break the eggs into a bowl, season and beat well. Add the cream and milk, mix together, and pour into each flan. Bake for about 20 minutes until just set. Remove from the oven and allow to cool a little before serving. Decorate with a few sprigs of parsley.

LEICESTER DOUGHNUTS WITH SPICED CELERY SAUCE

I come from the English shires, not far from Melton Mowbray where Leicester cheese has its origins, and I was regularly given this nutty-flavoured cheese, grilled on toast, on my return from a cold, wet paper-round. I still enjoy its rich, mellow flavour in the form of these rather unusual doughnuts. They require a strongly flavoured, mature cheese: anything less will result in a bland lump of fried dough. This is not a recipe for plastic-wrapped cheese which has little or no flavour. Use a farmhouse cheese cut from a mature truckle with a firm rind. The longer this cheese is kept, the nuttier its flavour will become, so this recipe is ideal for using leftovers.

SERVES 6 AS AN APPETIZER

250g/8oz self-raising flour
salt and freshly ground black pepper
125g/4oz red Leicester cheese, grated
30g/1oz unsalted butter, cut into small pieces
1 small free-range egg
90ml/3fl oz milk
oil for deep-frying (see pages xii–xiii)

FOR THE SPICED CELERY SAUCE:
4 tablespoons olive or vegetable oil
125g/4oz celery, finely chopped
2 small spring onions, chopped
¼ teaspoon coriander seeds
¼ teaspoon cayenne pepper
¼ teaspoon ground cumin
¼ teaspoon chilli powder
salt and freshly ground black pepper
150ml/5fl oz single cream or crème fraîche

First make the sauce: put the oil into a frying pan and add the celery and spring onion. Cook until soft. Add the spices, salt and pepper and cook for a couple of minutes. Remove from the heat and transfer to a bowl to cool slightly.

Then make the doughnuts: sift the flour with salt and pepper into a food-processor bowl. Add the cheese and butter and blend until smooth. Beat the egg into the milk and add to the flour and cheese mixture. Blend the dough – it should be fairly soft but holding its shape. Add a little more milk if you feel it necessary. (To make the doughnuts by hand, blend the cheese and butter together using a fork, then add the dry ingredients, then the egg and milk.) Deep-fry in teaspoon amounts in very hot oil until golden-brown and crisp, turning frequently for even cooking. Stir the cream or crème fraîche into the spiced celery sauce and serve with the doughnuts.

BACON AND SORREL
POTATO PATTIES

These little potato patties make a delicious breakfast dish served with fried eggs and bacon. I think it is a shame that so few people have time for a proper breakfast these days. We always have a cooked breakfast of some kind. It provides a harmonious start to the day, slows us down and puts us in a good frame of mind. Breakfast is not so easy for those who have to get families ready and then be at work on time themselves, but it is a good thing to make time for it if you can. Breakfast is when we can allow ourselves a little space, while the remainder of the day is for others. The patties can be made ahead of time and stored in clingfilm in the refrigerator until required (up to 2 days). Serve with crispy bacon, free-range fried or scrambled egg, and, if really hungry, fried bread, sausages, mushrooms and tomatoes.

SERVES 4

4 tablespoons olive oil
6 large shallots, peeled and chopped
125g/4oz smoked streaky bacon, rind removed, finely chopped
60g/2oz fresh sorrel leaves, shredded
500g/1lb potatoes, boiled and mashed
¼ nutmeg, freshly grated
175g/6oz fresh Parmesan cheese, finely grated
salt and freshly ground black pepper
¼ teaspoon cayenne pepper
1 free-range egg, beaten
a little flour for dusting before frying
a little vegetable oil for frying

Heat the olive oil in a frying pan. Add the shallots and cook gently until just softening. Add the bacon and cook until the bacon is done. Put in the sorrel leaves, stir for a few seconds, then remove the pan from the heat and tip the mixture into a bowl. Add the mashed potato, nutmeg, Parmesan, salt, pepper and cayenne pepper. Blend all the ingredients together thoroughly. Bind together with the beaten egg. Form into evenly shaped patties, dust with a little flour and put into a suitable container until needed.

When required, remove the patties, heat a little vegetable oil in a frying pan, and fry the patties on both sides until golden-brown.

PEPPERED PORK COUNTRY PÂTÉ

Our restaurant was featured in an article in a Sunday paper, and this pâté was enjoyed by the food writer/critic who wrote the piece. The only thing he did not like was the dish's name, and suggested that 'country' pâté brought to mind supermarket packaging. The word 'country', referring to pâté, does of course mean 'of a coarse consistency', and the real problem here is that the supermarkets have latched on to rural words in their quest to convince customers that their products have just been made in a farmhouse by a jolly farmer's wife or a dairy maid. This is a wonderful pâté and fairly easy to make. The peach and apple chutney (page 259) and the harvest chutney (page 260) are excellent accompaniments, along with a chunk of homemade bread and a green salad.

SERVES 8 to 10

1.5kg/3lb piece belly of pork, skin removed, minced (a butcher will do this for you)
125g/4oz smoked streaky bacon, rind removed, finely chopped
2 small onions, peeled and chopped
2 teaspoons ground allspice
2 teaspoons ground ginger
small bunch fresh thyme, stems removed
1 clove garlic, crushed with a little salt
1 tablespoon green peppercorns
90ml/3fl oz brandy
freshly ground black pepper
2 small free-range eggs, beaten
250g/8oz smoked streaky bacon, rind removed, to line loaf tins
2 bay leaves

Preheat the oven to 180°C/350°F/gas 4.

Put the minced pork into a large mixing bowl. Put the bacon and onion into a food processor and blend for about 1 minute, then turn out and mix with the pork. Add the allspice, ginger, thyme, garlic, peppercorns, brandy and pepper. Stir in the beaten eggs and blend thoroughly together.

Line 2 × 500g/1lb loaf tins with the streaky bacon, put a bay leaf into each tin and spoon in the pâté mixture. Cover tightly with kitchen foil and stand the loaf tins in a roasting pan. Pour in boiling water to come halfway up the sides of the tins. Cook in the preheated oven for 2½ hours, topping up the water if necessary from time to time. Test by inserting a skewer into the centre of the pâté: if the juices are still pink, the pâté is not ready; if the juices run clear, it is.

When cooked through, remove the loaf tins from the water and allow to cool, then put into the refrigerator and leave overnight. Next day turn out the pâté, wrap in clingfilm and store in the refrigerator until needed. (Sealed well, it keeps for 3 days. You can also freeze the pâté.)

To serve, slice thinly and accompany with one or both of the chutneys as suggested above.

HAM AND APPLE PASTIES

When Angela's sisters were small, we would pack our vintage Austin 8 with pies and salads and take a picnic on to the Marlborough Downs. The old car was named Dot, that being the lettering on the registration plate. It was an open-top model and when travelling with the hood down and a car full of food, children and dogs, it felt a bit like travelling with Noddy (no offence to the driver). These little pasties are ideal for picnics, lunch or supper, since they can be eaten hot or cold. If eaten hot at home, serve with an apple sauce or with spicy tomato sauce (page 247) and fresh vegetables.

MAKES 6

60g/2oz unsalted butter
1 large onion, peeled and finely chopped
3 eating apples, peeled, cored and chopped
250g/8oz ham, diced
30g/1oz fresh Parmesan cheese, grated
salt and freshly ground black pepper
1 teaspoon cayenne pepper
1 teaspoon chopped fresh tarragon
1½lb/750g wholemeal shortcrust pastry (page 234)
beaten egg to glaze

Melt the butter in a frying pan and add the onion. Fry until soft, then add the apple and cook for a further 2 minutes.

Put the cooked onion and apple into a large mixing bowl and allow to cool a little. Add the ham, Parmesan cheese, seasonings and tarragon, and blend all the ingredients well.

Preheat the oven to 200°C/400°F/gas 6.

Remove the prepared pastry from the refrigerator and divide into 6 equal pieces. Roll out into circles. Place a little of the ham and apple mixture on the centre of one circle, and continue until the mixture is evenly distributed among all the circles.

Take the bottom edge of the pastry and fold it over until it meets the top edge. Pinch the edges together to seal. This stage must be done carefully; if it is hurried, the pastry may break up and the pasties will split in the oven.

Place the pasties on a greased baking tray, brush over with beaten egg and bake in the preheated oven for 20 to 25 minutes. Then reduce the heat to 160°C/325°F/gas 3 and bake for a further 15 minutes.

BACON PASTIES

Before the First World War, bacon or pork was the usual meat eaten in the English countryside, and beef or mutton was reserved for harvest celebrations or other special occasions. Most villagers kept at least one pig and held this versatile animal in high esteem. In some places he was called 'the gentleman who paid the rent' because you could use every part of the pig except the grunt. Cooked meat and fruit wrapped in pastry was first made for farm workers to take to the fields and was eaten around noon, sitting under a hedge or a shady tree. Food does not need to be foreign or exotic in order to taste good and be acceptable on the dining table. These pasties can be 'dressed up' to look their best at a supper party or they can 'come as they are' for picnics, lunch, or high tea. To dress them up, decorate the pasties before cooking with pastry leaves firmly fixed to the fluted edge of the pasty. At the serving stage, arrange sprigs of fresh parsley at either end of the pasty and serve with a creamy mushroom sauce, creamed potatoes, butter-glazed carrots and runner beans or peas. These pasties are easy for children to prepare if they have a little help in frying the bacon and moving the pasties in and out of the oven. At the prepared but uncooked stage, the pasties can be frozen until required. Allow to thaw, then bake as described in the recipe.

MAKES 6

a little oil for frying the bacon
175g/6oz smoked streaky bacon, rind removed, cut into small pieces
2 sticks celery, diced
125g/4oz cooked potato, diced
2 spring onions, cut into small rings
1 cooked carrot, diced
salt and freshly ground black pepper
500g/1lb wholemeal shortcrust pastry (page 234)
milk for brushing

Preheat the oven to 220°C/425°F/gas 7.

Heat the oil in a frying pan and fry the bacon. Add the celery, potato, onion and carrot. Stir for a couple of minutes until the vegetables are tender, then remove from the heat. Season to taste.

Remove the prepared pastry from the refrigerator and roll out. Cut into 6 rounds using a saucer or small saucepan lid as a cutter. Place a portion of the vegetable and bacon mixture in the centre of each circle of pastry. Lightly dampen the edges of the pastry, then draw them up and press firmly together with your fingers. If you have the time, form leaves from any leftover pastry and fix them firmly on to the pasty near the fluted edge. Brush the pastry all over with a little milk. Place the pasties on a baking tray and bake towards the top of the preheated oven for about 20 minutes until the pastry begins to brown.

Remove from the oven, place on a warmed serving dish and serve with vegetables or a green salad.

3

Fish

SALMON CRUMBLE

A slightly unusual way of serving salmon, instead of the regular poached or grilled. We serve this crumble as a first course or, with double quantities, as a main dish. Among our regular customers we have one family whose young teenage daughter insists upon having this as her main course each time she comes to the restaurant.

SERVES 6 to 8 AS A STARTER, 4 AS A MAIN COURSE

60g/2oz unsalted butter
1 onion, peeled and finely chopped
30g/1oz plain flour
300ml/10fl oz milk
2 teaspoons anchovy essence, or 1 tin anchovy fillets, drained, soaked in
90ml/3fl oz milk and chopped
2 teaspoons tomato purée
freshly ground black pepper
120ml/4fl oz double cream
30g/1oz fresh parsley, chopped
500g/1lb cooked salmon, skin and bones removed
90g/3oz wholemeal breadcrumbs mixed with 3 teaspoons vegetable oil

Preheat the oven to 190°C/375°F/gas 5.

Put half the butter into a saucepan with the onion and cook until soft. Remove the onion and set aside. Add the remaining butter to the pan, melt, and mix in the flour. Cook for 2 minutes, then gradually add the milk, stirring well. Return the onion to the pan. Add the anchovy essence or anchovies to the pan. Stir in the tomato purée, pepper (you probably will not need salt as the anchovy is already salty – taste to check), cream and parsley. Flake the salmon and fold it into the cream mixture. Pour into an ovenproof dish. Spread the breadcrumbs over the top and bake in the preheated oven for 30 to 35 minutes until the top is nicely browned and crunchy.

CHILLED SALMON SOUFFLÉ

Once, during our outside catering days, we did a cold summer buffet in a large country house near Cheltenham. All the food was arranged on the long, cloth-covered table. We had to leave the room for a couple of minutes, and on our return found the hostess's six-year-old son kicking his football at the buffet table to see if he could knock the soufflés and gâteaux off. I hurried forward, picked up little 'George', stuffed him under my arm, confiscated the football and carried him off to his nursery, where I locked him in. We did let him out eventually, after hearing his mother calling him for his tea. Fortunately, his aim was not good. This was one of the soufflés made specially for the occasion. Soufflés have an unjustified reputation for being difficult to make. For this dish it is especially important to use very fresh eggs, free-range, please. The soufflé is ideal for a main course for a buffet, lunch or dinner party, whatever the season.

SERVES 4 to 6

450ml/15fl oz milk
1 shallot, peeled and sliced
1 small carrot, cut into strips
2 cloves
½ bay leaf
4 black peppercorns, crushed
300g/10oz fresh salmon, skin and bones removed (or trout fillets if preferred)
45g/1½oz unsalted butter
45g/1½oz plain flour
2 large free-range eggs, separated
2 teaspoons anchovy essence
2 teaspoons tomato purée
1 teaspoon fresh tarragon, snipped with scissors
grated rind and juice of 1 lemon

salt and freshly ground black pepper
15g/½oz gelatine, dissolved in 150ml/5fl oz water
150ml/5fl oz double cream
slices of cucumber and lemon and a few sprigs fresh parsley to garnish

Put the milk, shallot, carrot, cloves, bay leaf and peppercorns into a saucepan. Simmer for 2 to 3 minutes, but do not boil. Turn off the heat and allow the milk to infuse for 15 minutes.

Strain the milk into a saucepan and put in the salmon, discarding the vegetables, bay leaf and spices. Poach for 5 minutes. Remove the fish, and set aside the liquid after checking that you have 450ml/15fl oz (make up with a little milk if necessary). Pound the salmon until it is smooth and free of lumps or flakes so that it will blend properly into the sauce, and set aside.

Melt the butter in a saucepan. Add the flour and cook for a couple of minutes. Remove from the heat and gradually blend in the poaching milk, beating well in as you do so. Continue beating and pouring until all the liquid is blended in. Return to the heat and cook for a further 2 minutes, beating well. Remove once more from the heat and beat in the egg yolks. Then add the anchovy essence, tomato purée, tarragon, lemon rind and juice, and seasonings. Blend well in, pour into a bowl and allow to cool.

Prepare a 600ml/1-pint soufflé dish as described on page xiv.

Make sure the gelatine has completely dissolved in the water. If necessary, place the basin in a saucepan of hot water until the gelatine has dissolved. Stir into the sauce mixture. Fold the pounded fish into the sauce. Next whip the cream until it just holds its shape and stands in soft peaks, then fold it into the sauce. Whisk the egg whites stiffly and fold these also into the sauce. Pour the mixture into the prepared soufflé dish and chill in the refrigerator until set (at least 3 hours or overnight).

When required, peel away the paper and decorate the top of the soufflé with the cucumber and lemon slices and sprigs of parsley.

OAK-SMOKED SALMON CHEESECAKE

This rather unusual cheesecake is ideal for a party, which is why the ingredients are in such large quantities. It is very rich, and guests will not need too large a slice. Purchase a well-flavoured smoked salmon because ordinary smoked salmon is too bland – when you find some really good smoked salmon, there is all the more reason for making a party out of it. We use oak-smoked salmon from the Minola smokehouses in Lechlade, Gloucestershire.

SERVES 14 to 16

FOR THE BASE:
150g/5oz wholemeal crackers
1 packet Ritz crackers
125g/4oz butter

FOR THE TOPPING:
600g/1¼lb oak-smoked salmon
2 × 200g/7oz packets cream cheese
500g/1lb natural yoghurt
finely grated rind and juice of 1 lemon
freshly ground white pepper
small bunch fresh chives, finely chopped
6 rounded teaspoons powdered gelatine, dissolved in 300ml/10fl oz cold water
slices of lemon and sprigs of fresh parsley to garnish

First make the base: finely crumble the crackers by using a few turns of the processor blade or by wrapping them in a clean cloth and crushing with a rolling pin. Melt the butter in a saucepan and blend in the crumbs. When the crumbs have completely blended with the butter, use a palette knife or the back of a tablespoon to press the crumbs on to the base of a 25cm/10-inch diameter loose-based cake tin, easing the mixture about 2.5cm/1 inch up the side of the tin. Put into the refrigerator to set the butter.

To make the cheesecake, first remove any skin from the smoked salmon, then put the salmon into a food processor or liquidizer and blend until smooth. Add the cream cheese, yoghurt, lemon rind and juice, and pepper to taste. Blend together thoroughly. Pour into a bowl and sprinkle in the chives. Make sure the gelatine has completely dissolved in the water, then pour into the cheesecake mixture and blend well. Pour on to the biscuit base and chill in the refrigerator for 3 to 4 hours.

Before serving, gently remove the cheesecake from the tin. Decorate with twists of fresh lemon and a few sprigs of parsley.

SALMON À LA HALL
(Salmon with Tomato and Vanilla Mirepoix)

We received a telephone call one Saturday night from one of our most regular customers, wanting to book a table for Sunday lunch. His wife was not long out of hospital and needed a good meal, and the poor man himself had had a fall down the stairs, so they both needed some tender loving care. As it turned out, being a wet February Sunday, we had no other bookings, so the Halls joined us for lunch in our kitchen. This is what we ate, and the recipe is dedicated to them, our dear and loyal friends.

SERVES 4

8 fresh asparagus spears
120ml/4fl oz vegetable oil
2 large shallots, peeled and finely chopped
8 tomatoes, skinned (page 12), deseeded and chopped
½ vanilla pod, split into two lengthways
1 teaspoon caster sugar
4 fresh salmon fillets, skin and bones removed
sea salt and freshly ground black pepper
a little chopped fresh parsley to garnish

FOR THE SAUCE:
good handful chopped fresh chives
150ml/5fl oz single cream
60g/2oz unsalted butter
180ml/6fl oz milk

Trim away any woody stems from the base of the asparagus.

Heat the oil in a frying pan and lightly sauté the shallot until soft. Add the tomato, scrape the vanilla seeds from the pods into the tomato, and put in the pods themselves and the sugar. Cook over a very low heat for a few minutes to dissolve the sugar. Remove from the heat and take out the vanilla pods. (Wash the vanilla pods, allow to dry and place in a jar of caster sugar for vanilla sugar if you wish.) Set the tomato and vanilla mirepoix aside.

Put the salmon into a steamer, season with a little salt and pepper and steam for about 5 minutes. The exact time will depend on the thickness of the fillets. Test if the fish is cooked by gently pulling apart the thickest part; if it still looks raw, steam for a little longer, but take care not to overcook. Two minutes before the end of steaming time, add the asparagus to the steamer.

To make the sauce: put the chives, cream, butter, milk and seasonings into a small saucepan. Bring to simmering point and stir for a couple of minutes. Remove from the heat.

Gently warm through the tomato and vanilla mirepoix. Place a fillet of steamed salmon on each warmed dinner plate. Mound a spoonful of the mirepoix on top of each fillet, pour the sauce around, sprinkle the parsley over, and arrange 2 asparagus spears alongside. Serve at once.

CRAB AND HERB CREAM TARTLETS

A cookery writer friend, who champions the cause of British cookery and fresh, natural produce, wanted the recipe for these little crab tartlets. Angela offered to give her the recipe there and then, but she, a true author, said she would wait to see it in the book. So here it is, with many thanks for her patience. We intended the tartlets to be a first course but are quite often asked to serve them as a main dish, so we do, and then we serve two per person. We use fresh Cornish crab but, if you are feeling extravagant, substitute fresh lobster meat. The tartlets must not be overheated at the final stage of cooking, because the delicate flavours can lose their freshness. We accompany this dish with a well-seasoned cucumber and dill salad bound together with natural yoghurt.

SERVES 4 AS A STARTER, 2 AS A MAIN COURSE

250g/8oz Cheddar cheese pastry (page 235)
small bunch fresh chives
small bunch fresh tarragon
120ml/4fl oz natural yoghurt
240ml/8fl oz double cream
grated rind and juice of 1 small lemon
2 teaspoons sugar
sea salt and freshly ground black pepper
good shake of cayenne pepper
1 large dressed crab

Preheat the oven to 190°C/375°F/gas 5.

Roll out the pastry and cut out 4 equal circles. Press into a patty tin and bake blind until a pale golden colour.

Put all the ingredients except the crabmeat into a food processor and blend together until smooth. Pour into a basin.

Remove the crabmeat from the shell and put the meat into a bowl. Fold in 4 level tablespoons of the blended herb cream and mix well with the crabmeat. Put the baked tartlet cases on to a baking tray and divide the crab mixture evenly between them. Spoon herb cream over each one.

Bake the crab tartlets in the preheated oven for 10 to 15 minutes until heated through. Spoon over any remaining herb cream and serve at once.

SALMON CREAM PIE

Many a groan is heard when 'Fish pie' is the answer to 'What's for supper?'. This recipe is an antidote to the usual fish pie. It is very easy to make and is ideal for family meals as well as for entertaining. Serve with fresh green vegetables or a green salad. You can even cheat (as if you would!) and use tinned salmon if fresh is not available.

SERVES 4 to 6

250g/8oz salmon
300ml/10fl oz béchamel sauce (page 240)
2 teaspoons tomato purée
2 large hard-boiled free-range eggs, chopped
1 teaspoon anchovy essence
salt and freshly ground white pepper
1kg/2lb potatoes, boiled and creamed with butter and milk, and well seasoned, especially with pepper
melted butter to brush over the potato
sprigs fresh parsley and slices of lemon and cucumber to garnish

Preheat the oven to 180°C/350°F/gas 4.

Flake the salmon and mix with the béchamel sauce. Add the tomato purée, chopped egg and anchovy essence. Mix well and season to taste. Pile into an ovenproof dish and spread the creamed potato on top of the fish mixture. Fork up the potato to give a crunchy top. Brush over with the melted butter and bake in the preheated oven for 30 to 35 minutes, until the mixture is cooked in the centre and the top is golden-brown. If the dish is deep, it will take longer to cook through at the centre, while a shallower dish will naturally take a shorter time. Serve garnished with sprigs of parsley and twists of lemon and cucumber.

KIPPER PATÉ WITH WHISKY AND FRESH LIME

Kipper pâté is quite usual, but the addition of lime juice and whisky turns it into something more special. The whisky is optional, but if you do use it, allow the pâté to mature overnight, or better still for 24 hours. To make clarified butter: melt butter in a saucepan over a very gentle heat without stirring. Skim the surface of the melted butter with a spoon or a piece of kitchen paper to remove the foam. Carefully pour the skimmed butter into a clean bowl, leaving the whitish sediment at the bottom of the saucepan. Keep in the refrigerator until required.

SERVES 4

4 kipper fillets
30ml/1fl oz whisky or Drambuie (optional)
60g/2oz butter, melted
4 tablespoons natural yoghurt
cayenne pepper
grated rind and juice of 1 lime
clarified butter (see introduction above; optional)
sprigs fresh parsley and thin slices of lime to garnish (optional)

Poach the kipper fillets in a little water until just cooked. This will take about 3 minutes. Strain and remove any skin and bones. Liquidize the fillets with the whisky, if using, the butter, yoghurt, cayenne pepper, and lime rind and juice. When the mixture is smooth, pour into one large or several small serving pots and allow to cool. When cold, cover with the clarified butter, if using, and refrigerate until required. If the pâté is to be eaten straight away and clarified butter is not used, garnish with parsley sprigs and thin slices of lime.

DEVILLED CRAB

Emile Jung, one of the great chefs of Alsace, sums up our feelings on what running a restaurant is all about. He says in 'Les Grandes Tables d'Alsace' (in *A Taste of Alsace* by Sue Style): 'We are in the business of happiness, purveyors of pleasure, by appointment to the people.' The production of a good meal is more than technical expertise. It is also more, much more, than the unpacking of ready-made catering dishes. We recently received a brochure from one of the larger catering companies advertising their 'boil in the bag' and portion-control packs and exclaiming, in large full-colour print, 'De-skill your kitchen.' We cannot believe that anyone running a restaurant would wish to employ a kitchen assistant whose only skill is unpacking. This crab dish is hearty and warming, as well as delicious, just right for a chilly evening, summer or winter. It is a quick and easy dish and can be prepared in advance up to the grilling stage. When required, dot with the butter and pop under the grill for a few minutes.

SERVES 6 to 8

90g/3oz unsalted butter
1 large onion, peeled and finely chopped
500g/1lb crabmeat
1 teaspoon curry paste per person
175g/6oz wholemeal breadcrumbs
2 level tablespoons tomato purée
2 tablespoons Worcestershire sauce
1 tablespoon anchovy essence
grated rind and juice of 1 lemon
salt and freshly ground black pepper
180ml/6fl oz single cream
grated Cheddar cheese for the topping
6 or 8 small knobs of butter for grilling
slices of lemon and fresh parsley sprigs to garnish

Melt the butter in a saucepan. Add the onion and cook until soft.

Put the crabmeat into a large bowl. Add the cooked onion, curry paste, breadcrumbs, tomato purée, Worcestershire sauce, anchovy essence, and lemon rind and juice. Season to taste and mix all the ingredients together, making sure the curry paste is well blended in. Fold in the cream and spoon the mixture into 6 to 8 ovenproof ramekins. Sprinkle a little grated Cheddar cheese over each. Place a small knob of butter on top of the crab and put under a hot grill until golden brown. Serve garnished with a twist of lemon and a sprig of parsley.

SMOKED HADDOCK AND PRAWN TERRINE

To celebrate our first six months at the Loaves and Fishes in Burbage, we held a garden party for 36 guests. We hired the local scout 'marquee', which was a large green ex-army supply tent. Our guests loved it because it reminded them of their service days, when they had lived in these tents during the war in India or Egypt. A clarinet trio played in the background and the sun shone warmly and brightly – a lovely way to spend a summer Sunday. The cold buffet included this fish terrine. For best results use natural smoked haddock, not the dyed, bright yellow variety.

SERVES 4 to 6

350g/12oz natural oak-smoked haddock
150ml/5fl oz milk
30g/1oz butter
30g/1oz plain flour
2 teaspoons anchovy essence
grated rind and juice of ½ lemon
150ml/5fl oz double cream
salt and freshly ground black pepper
3 rounded teaspoons powdered gelatine, dissolved in
180ml/6fl oz cold water
125g/4oz peeled prawns
slices of lemon to garnish

Skin the haddock and remove any bones. Put the milk into a pan, add the haddock and poach for 10 to 15 minutes. When cooked, remove the fish from the milk and reserve the poaching liquid. Melt the butter in a saucepan, add the flour and cook for a couple of minutes. Gradually pour the milk into the saucepan and beat well in until you have a thick sauce. Add the anchovy essence, lemon rind and juice, cream and seasonings. Pour in the dissolved gelatine, stirring all the time. Put the contents of the saucepan into a food processor along with the haddock and blend until smooth. Pour the mixture into a mixing bowl and stir in the prawns. Check the seasonings, pour into individual ramekins and chill in the refrigerator until set (at least 3 hours). Before serving, garnish with twists of fresh lemon.

FISH QUENELLES WITH
ORANGE SAUCE

Quenelles are small dumplings made from minced meat or fish that is bound with egg whites and cream and then poached and served with a cream sauce. They were once extremely popular and could be found regularly on the menus of restaurants and hotel dining rooms during the first half of the twentieth century. Some of you may remember Pruniers, one of the finest fish restaurants in London. Madam Prunier was a dear friend of Angela's great aunt Iris Syrett, who founded the Tante Marie School of Cookery, which was opened by Madam Prunier in the early 1950s. These quenelles would certainly have been on the menu at that marvellous establishment, which closed its doors after 64 years in 1989 but has now reopened in Paris as Maison Prunier. To serve as a main course, large quenelles are made; for a first course, smaller ones. Tiny quenelles can be made for garnishing soups and stews. The secret is to make sure all the ingredients are well chilled before being used, and then quenelles are not as difficult to make as you may think. We would like to see them appear in restaurants more often – they are not only delicious but ideal for the weight-conscious. For this recipe we have used economical whiting fillets, but for a special dinner party we would use fresh salmon or trout.

2 free-range egg whites
500g / 1lb whiting fillets, skinned, broken into small pieces
120ml / 4fl oz double cream
salt and freshly ground white pepper
1 recipe quantity fresh orange sauce (page 248)

Blend the egg whites and fish until smooth in a food processor or blender, then add the cream and seasonings. The mixture is fairly heavy so it may have to be blended in batches. Chill in the refrigerator for at least 1 hour, longer if possible.

When required, form the quenelle mixture into egg shapes: use 2 tablespoons dipped in hot water and scoop the mixture from one spoon to the other. Poach in salted, simmering (not boiling) water for 10 to 15 minutes. Remove carefully and keep warm in a bowl of hot water. When all the quenelles are cooked, drain well and place on a warmed serving dish. Spoon over the orange sauce and serve.

FRESH TROUT
CROQUETTES

These tasty croquettes are an ideal way of using up leftover fish, although if you do not have any, it is worth buying some fresh specially to make them. Almost any type of minced fish can be used. We make this versatile dish for breakfast, as well as serving it as a first course, and as a main dish with an egg and parsley sauce (made from chopped hard-boiled eggs and parsley mixed with equal parts of béchamel sauce and double cream with seasoning). Tiny croquettes can be used for garnishing dishes, or can even be served as an hors d'oeuvre. They freeze well, so can be made at any time and kept as a useful standby.

SERVES 4

500g/1lb fresh trout, cleaned and gutted if not using leftovers or fillets
250g/8oz potatoes, peeled and diced
medium bunch watercress, stalks removed, finely chopped
30g/1oz butter
salt and freshly ground black pepper
1 free-range egg
oil for deep-frying (see pages xii–xiii)

FOR COATING:
2 tablespoons seasoned plain flour
1 free-range egg, beaten
white or wholemeal breadcrumbs

Place the trout in a steamer and steam for 15 minutes. When cooked, remove the skin and bones and flake the fish with a fork.

Cook the potatoes in a saucepan of boiling, salted water until just tender. Drain and pass through a sieve or potato ricer. Add the chopped watercress.

Mix the fish with the potato and watercress. Add the butter, season to taste, then add the egg and beat well.

Form the mixture into croquettes. Roll them in the seasoned flour, coat with the beaten egg and breadcrumbs, then deep-fry for about 3 minutes until golden-brown. Drain on absorbent paper and serve.

FILLETS OF TROUT
WITH FRESH DILL
AND SPINACH SAUCE

'The silver scaled fish that softly swim/Within the sweet brook's crystal watery stream,' wrote Izaak Walton in the seventeenth century. It is a perfect description of 'the lazy trout' so sadly declining in our local River Kennet while nearby Swindon town takes the water for its ever-growing population and industry. You can, however, buy good fresh trout from supermarkets, fishmongers and game butchers. Select bright-eyed fish, checking that the gills are a bright red, and that the flesh is firm to the touch and its colour a healthy pink. Take care – some supermarkets remove the gills, making it difficult to tell the age and freshness of the fish. They may believe this is part of the cleaning and gutting process. Never buy a flabby, dull-looking fish of any variety. Trout can be bought ready-filleted, which saves a lot of time and also allows you to see the colour of the flesh at a glance.

SERVES 2

2 trout fillets, skin and bones removed
1 tablespoon seasoned plain flour
30g/1oz unsalted butter
1 tablespoon chopped fresh chives
small bunch fresh dill, snipped into small pieces
good handful fresh spinach leaves, shredded
120ml/4fl oz dry white wine
120ml/4fl oz single cream
sprigs fresh dill or parsley and/or chopped chives to garnish

Toss the trout fillets in the seasoned flour. Melt the butter in a frying pan over a low heat, add the floured fillets and seal them for a couple of minutes on each side. Sprinkle in the chives, dill and spinach. Pour in the wine and cream and cover. Cook for about 4 minutes over a very low heat. The exact time will depend upon the thickness of the fillets.

When cooked, remove the fillets from the pan and place on a warmed serving dish. Stir the sauce in the pan to blend the juices. Season well to taste and pour the sauce over the trout. Decorate with a few sprigs of dill or parsley and/or sprinkle over chives. Serve with a fresh green salad and boiled new potatoes.

TROUT FILLETS IN PUFF PASTRY

This recipe has become something of a trade mark in our restaurant. The fish in pastry is meltingly flavoursome and looks wonderful arranged simply on a pretty serving plate (see the book's cover, and we hope you agree). We explain here how to skin the fillets, but far easier is to ask the fishmonger to skin them for you. The dish then becomes very quick to prepare. The pastry fish can also be made in advance and frozen until required (remove from the freezer about 30 minutes before glazing and cooking). Serve with a tossed green salad and spicy tomato sauce (page 247) or one of the spring onion sauces (pages 244–5).

SERVES 4

4 × 125g/4oz trout fillets
500g/1lb puff pastry
sea salt and freshly ground black pepper
1 teaspoon chopped fresh tarragon leaves
beaten egg, to glaze

Remove the skin from the trout: place the fillets skin-side down on a board or marble slab. You need a sharp, broad-bladed knife. Take hold of a piece of skin at one end of the fillet and place the knife blade under the flesh just above the skin. With a sawing action away from your body, gently saw the flesh from the skin. Check the skinned fillets and remove any bones if necessary.

Preheat the oven to 200°C/400°F/gas 6.

Roll out the pastry. Cut into 4 rectangles a little longer than each fillet and wide enough to envelope the fish completely. Place a fillet in the centre of each piece of pastry. Season to taste and sprinkle with the tarragon. Wrap the pastry around each fish then turn over so that the seams are underneath. Form into a fish shape with a tail. Use a skewer or the point of a sharp knife to create an eye and scales. If desired, make a pastry fin, but cook this separately (or it will burn before the fish is ready) and put it into place when the fish is cooked. Brush the pastry all over with beaten egg, place on a damp baking tray and bake in the preheated oven until golden-brown, checking the colour from time to time and remembering to remove the fin early. When the pastry enclosing the fillet has turned golden-brown (about 14 minutes), the fish will be cooked. Serve at once.

FILLETS OF PLAICE WITH LIME AND BASIL BUTTER SAUCE

This is a super dish, suitable as a first course with one small fillet for each person, or as a main course with one large or two small fillets per person. The sauce is refreshing, and the dish pleases the eye as well as the tastebuds.

SERVES 4 AS A STARTER, 2 AS A MAIN COURSE

2 large or 4 small fresh plaice fillets
a few knobs of butter for grilling
sea salt and freshly ground black pepper
chopped fresh parsley or basil and slices of lemon and lime to garnish

FOR THE SAUCE:
grated rind and juice of 1 large lime
120ml/4fl oz fish stock or water
4 tablespoons dry vermouth
1 teaspoon clear honey
125g/4oz unsalted butter, cut into small cubes
10 leaves fresh basil, cut into tiny pieces
90ml/3fl oz double cream

First make the sauce: put the lime rind and juice into a saucepan, pour in the stock or water, vermouth and honey, stir and bring to the boil. Cook until the liquid is reduced by about one third. Then turn the heat right down and whisk in the butter until completely blended in. Do not boil the sauce at this stage. Sprinkle in the basil leaves, pour in the cream and stir well. Keep the sauce warm while you grill the fish.

Put the fillets skin-side down on the wire rack of a grill pan and pour a tiny amount of water into the bottom of the pan. This produces a little steam to prevent the plaice from drying out. Dot the fish with the butter, season to taste and put under a preheated moderate grill for 2 to 3 minutes, turning the fillets over halfway through grilling time. Exact grilling time depends upon the thickness of the fillets. When the plaice is ready, peel away the skin from the fillets and put the fish on a warmed serving dish or dinner plates. Spoon over the warm sauce, garnish with parsley or basil and twists of lemon and lime, and serve.

PLAICE AND SPINACH PARCELS

The only time Angela and I split our working partnership was many years ago when we were asked to do a buffet lunch for a high-society wedding on the same day that Angela had agreed to do a shooting lunch for a long-standing client some 10 miles away. A hundred and eighty wedding guests were due to arrive at 12.30 p.m. for a cold buffet. On the day I needed only to set out the already prepared food, and leave the rest of the work to the household staff. It should have gone smoothly: the guests were meant to be in the garden, library or hall, anywhere but the dining room which was the collection point for staff only. Lunch-time arrived, the food was set out, the household staff stood in line, and the nightmare began. Wedding guests surged in. I began putting food on to plates as fast as I was able, the staff distributing the plates as best they could. An hour later I was still serving the main dish and having to use the pudding plates. They disappeared and I started on the coffee saucers. Throughout all this I was opening and serving champagne, and when the champagne glasses ran out we resorted to port and sherry glasses. In the end we served nearly 300 guests. Angela arrived at three o'clock to help me – she thought – to serve the coffee and clear away the dishes, but I was still trying to serve main dishes, and was by now using up the supper food. What little food the last of the guests received was greeted with generous enthusiasm, with 'Thank you very much' and 'So kind'. I wanted to go home. Eventually this bad dream, as all bad dreams do, came to an end. The hostess apologized for the overwhelming number of guests and the mistake in numbers. We really had done a 'Loaves and Fishes'. We served fillet of plaice parcels on that fateful day. Here we have changed the recipe from cold poached plaice to breadcrumbed and deep-fried fillets. Serve with a sorrel or spinach sauce (page 246) or green pea and spring onion (page 244), accompanied by a fresh green salad and/or new potatoes. Perhaps you should make extra, in case of unexpected guests.

SERVES 8 AS A STARTER, 4 AS A MAIN COURSE

4 tablespoons olive oil
2 spring onions, finely chopped
250g/8oz fresh spinach, shredded
4 tablespoons water
8 fresh plaice fillets, any skin and bones removed
salt and freshly ground black pepper
freshly grated nutmeg
grated rind of 1 small lemon
150g/5oz fresh fine white breadcrumbs
2 free-range eggs, beaten
oil for deep-frying (see pages xii–xiii)

Pour the oil into a saucepan, add the spring onion and cook lightly for a couple of minutes. Then add the spinach and water and stir well into the oil and onion. Cover and cook for a few minutes until the spinach has reduced a little. Press down on the spinach in the pan with a fish slice to remove any excess liquid and then transfer it (with the spring onion) to a plate. Allow to cool a little, then, using scissors, chop the spinach and spring onion through. Divide evenly between the plaice fillets, season to taste with the salt, pepper and a little nutmeg, and roll up the fillets to form tight parcels. Tuck in the sides to keep the spinach in place.

Mix the lemon rind and the breadcrumbs together well. Dip the fillets into the beaten egg, then coat with the breadcrumbs. Repeat the process if there are any bare patches. Put the parcels on a tray and refrigerate, uncovered, for a few hours to firm them up. When required, deep-fry until golden-brown, then place in a low oven for a few minutes to keep warm and to ensure they are cooked right through. Serve, when ready, with your chosen sauce.

FILLETS OF SOLE WITH
FRESH PEAR AND TARRAGON
CREAM SAUCE

Midnight, and we were in Angela's old Morris Traveller. We called the car 'Chuggerbug' because it was and it did. We were dropping off our staff after a particularly busy Saturday night. Two of us sat in the back while Angela unloaded the napkins (the lady who washed up also washed and ironed the napkins) and a little fresh sole left over from the evening's menu, intended for the washing-up lady. While the unloading took place, Chuggerbug began a slow but steady move forwards. The handbrake, not brilliant at the best of times, had not been fully engaged, and the waitress and I, two bemused faces staring out of the window, began gliding forward down Rockley Lane into the dark and windy night. Angela, realizing that Chuggerbug was on the move, sprinted alongside the car and heaved open the door in an attempt to engage the handbrake. I tried to reach the brake from the back, but what with laughing and floundering over the back of the driver's seat, I was not successful. Angela, luckily, was. Now we cannot eat sole without remembering the runaway Chuggerbug and our washing-up lady standing in the middle of the dark lane laden with a huge basket of dirty napkins topped with a dish of sole fillets. This recipe is for a more peaceful experience. Firm, juicy pears are essential, the subtle flavours of the fruit and tarragon combining extremely well.

SERVES 8 AS A STARTER, 4 AS A MAIN COURSE

2 firm, not over-ripe, pears
8 fresh sole fillets, skinned and boned
slices of lemon and chopped fresh tarragon or parsley to garnish

FOR THE SAUCE:
4 free-range egg yolks
1 tablespoon caster sugar
90ml/3fl oz tarragon vinegar
2 tablespoons finely chopped fresh tarragon
90ml/3fl oz crème fraîche
salt and freshly ground white pepper

First begin to make the sauce: put the egg yolks, sugar, tarragon vinegar and tarragon into a saucepan. Stand the saucepan over another pan of hot water to make a bain-marie. Whisk the mixture until it reaches the consistency of custard, then remove from the heat. Set aside.

Peel and core the pears then cut each one into 4 slices. Wrap a fillet of sole around each slice of pear. Put the fish-and-pear parcels into a steamer and steam lightly for 4 to 5 minutes. Remove, place on a serving dish and allow to cool completely.

Whisk the crème fraîche into the sauce mixture and season to taste. Coat each sole fillet with the sauce and serve garnished with twists of lemon and a sprinkling of tarragon or parsley.

WHITING FILLETS WITH LIME OR LEMON HOLLANDAISE

This piquant sauce can accompany a variety of fish, such as salmon, sole or trout as well as whiting, and also goes well with fresh asparagus, baby leeks and broccoli. This recipe makes a regular appearance on our spring and summer menus as a first course, served with a fresh green salad. It is very popular with guests wanting a lighter diet. Hollandaise is served warm. If it becomes too hot, the sauce separates. Should this happen to you, remove the sauce from the heat and whisk in 1 to 2 tablespoons of ice-cold water until the sauce is smooth and creamy once more.

SERVES 4

FOR THE HOLLANDAISE:
2 free-range egg yolks
4 tablespoons tarragon vinegar
grated rind and juice of 1 lime or lemon
125g/4oz unsalted butter, cut into small pieces
salt and freshly ground black pepper

FOR THE FISH:
4 × 125g/4oz whiting fillets
a little melted butter for brushing
salt and freshly ground black pepper
1 tablespoon fresh tarragon, snipped with scissors
slices of lime or lemon to garnish

First make the hollandaise: put the egg yolks into a bowl and whisk in the vinegar and lime or lemon rind and juice. Put the bowl over a pan of hot water (the base must not touch the water) and heat, whisking gently all the time, until the mixture thickens. (Do not allow the water to go above simmering point.) Turn off the heat and gradually whisk the butter into the sauce. Season to taste. If the sauce is a little too sharp, add more butter. It should be slightly piquant, just thick enough to hold its shape, and should be served warm.

To prepare the whiting: put the fillets on to a grill pan and brush with the melted butter. Season to taste and place under a preheated moderate grill for about 5 minutes on each side. Thin fillets may need a little less time. Transfer to a warmed serving dish or dinner plates, and pour the warm hollandaise over. Sprinkle the tarragon over and garnish with a few slices of lime or lemon.

MONKFISH THERMIDOR

Because of the monkfish's bizarre appearance, usually only the tail finds its way to the fish markets. We needed a new fish dish to add to our menu and so decided to match monkfish, with its flavour reminiscent of lobster, with the classic lobster sauce, Thermidor. It works very well. A good Chardonnay is very important to the flavour of the sauce. We use an Australian Semillon Chardonnay or a Koonunga Hill, both of which are buttery with good lemony, oaky flavours that are imparted to the sauce. Breadcrumbs are another important ingredient. Homemade breadcrumbs have a good flavour, so, please, not the orange-coloured crumbs (how do they get to be that colour?) found in boxes. A green leaves and prawn salad and new potatoes are ideal accompaniments.

SERVES 4 to 6

300ml/10fl oz fish stock
150ml/5fl oz good Chardonnay
1 onion, peeled and chopped
6 black peppercorns, crushed
1 bay leaf
sprig fresh thyme
salt and freshly ground black pepper
450ml/15fl oz milk
1kg/2lb piece of monkfish tail, skinned and boned
125g/4oz unsalted butter
60g/2oz plain flour
1 teaspoon Dijon mustard
2 free-range egg yolks
150ml/5fl oz single cream
2 teaspoons lemon juice
90g/3oz fresh Parmesan cheese, grated
60g/2oz breadcrumbs

Boil together the stock and Chardonnay in a saucepan, then simmer to reduce to 150ml/5fl oz. Remove from the heat and reserve.

Put the onion, peppercorns, bay leaf, thyme, seasonings and milk into a saucepan. Bring to simmering point, then reduce the heat to very low. Cover, and cook for about 30 minutes so that the milk becomes infused with the herbs and seasonings.

While the milk is heating, cut the monkfish into bite-sized cubes. Melt half the butter in a heavy-based frying pan and cook the monkfish in small batches, turning constantly, for 3 to 4 minutes. When all the monkfish has been sautéed, set aside.

Remove the infused milk from the heat and strain into a bowl, discarding the ingredients left in the sieve. Melt the remaining butter in a saucepan and add the flour. Cook for a couple of minutes. Remove the pan from the heat and stir the infused, strained milk into the flour until the consistency is smooth. Return to the heat and bring to simmering point, stirring all the time, then pour in the prepared wine stock. Cook for 4 minutes, uncovered, until the sauce has thickened. Remove from the heat and allow to cool slightly. Stir in the mustard, egg yolks, cream and lemon juice. Do not allow to boil. Check the seasonings and add a little more salt and pepper if desired.

Divide the monkfish evenly into individual chafing dishes (shallow ovenproof dishes) or scallop shells if you have them. Pour the sauce equally between the dishes. Mix the Parmesan cheese with the breadcrumbs and sprinkle over the monkfish. Put under a preheated moderate grill and grill until golden-brown. Serve at once.

4
Meat

MEDALLIONS OF BEEF CHURCHILL
(Beef Fillets in Peppered Ham Sauce)

To celebrate our first year in our restaurant at Burbage, we put on a special dinner. As it was the fiftieth anniversary of VE Day, we had a band playing music from the 1940s. The menu included dishes such as salmon quenelles with a lobster and brandy sauce, meringue Lady Astor (white chocolate mousse inside a meringue swan with a pool of chocolate and vanilla sauce) and this recipe, medallions of beef Churchill. The evening went with a swing. Our guests came in their old service uniforms, some as air-raid wardens, others as the Home Guard, and a few complete with gas masks. The evening ended with a spirited rendering of the old war-time favourite 'We'll meet again'.

SERVES 4

45g/1½ oz butter
6 shallots, peeled and finely chopped
1 tablespoon plain flour
450ml/15fl oz beef or chicken stock
150ml/5fl oz medium-sweet white wine
2 teaspoons Dijon mustard
1 teaspoon black peppercorns, crushed
salt
175g/6oz peppered ham, cut into thin strips
150ml/5fl oz single cream
600g/1¼lb fillet of beef, in one piece and trimmed
a little oil for cooking the beef

Melt the butter in a saucepan, add the shallots, and cook until soft. Stir in the flour and cook for a few minutes. Pour in the stock gradually, beating as you go. Pour in the wine and add the mustard, peppercorns and a pinch of salt. Simmer for 10 minutes.

Add two-thirds of the ham and all of the cream to the sauce mixture, and stir well. Keep warm over a very low heat.

Cut the fillet of beef into thin slices and sauté in the oil according to your taste. Place the slices of cooked beef on a warmed serving plate, pour the sauce over, strew with the remaining strips of peppered ham and serve.

SUPREME OF CHICKEN WITH BASIL AND GOAT'S CHEESE

It was a hot summer Sunday. At the top end of our chapel restaurant the oak door stood open to let in the sunshine and air and to allow our guests to look across the fields to the Marlborough Downs shimmering in the distance. Angela and I were in the kitchen when we heard laughter coming from the restaurant, laughter which grew louder and louder until everyone there was roaring. We investigated and found to our horror that Daisy, our Saanen goat, had somehow managed to stretch her length of chain and walk up the stone steps leading into the restaurant, where she was casually nibbling the bark off the logs by the side of the wood-burning stove. Daisy was a great comedian who always played to an audience. Getting her back down the steps and outside was a comedy act in itself. She resisted our efforts to return her to her rightful place by standing on her hind legs and playfully butting us as we pushed and pulled her down the steps. Our guests fully appreciated the show and applauded Daisy as she made her unwilling exit, ears twitching, protesting loudly. Goat's cheese changes its character almost daily (as do goats themselves, as anyone who has kept them will know). Made from unpasteurized milk, it contains bacteria and enzymes which develop its unique flavour. The flavour varies also with the seasons, and goat's cheeses are at their best and most fragrant in the spring and summer, and turn more acid with the autumn and winter as the herbage becomes drier. For this recipe choose a well-flavoured cheese, full-bodied, soft and ripe.

SERVES 4

4 boneless free-range chicken breasts with skin attached
125g/4oz soft goat's cheese
1 small bunch fresh basil
salt and freshly ground black pepper

FOR THE SAUCE:
good handful fresh chives, finely chopped
150ml/5fl oz single cream
8 small leaves fresh basil, cut (at the last minute) into small pieces
salt and freshly ground black pepper

Cut a 4cm/1½-inch pocket in the side of each chicken breast. Cut the goat's cheese into 30g/1oz pieces and wrap a few basil leaves around each piece. Slot the basil and cheese inside the pocket of each chicken breast and close up gently. Lift a little of the skin on top of each chicken breast and slot 2 or 3 basil leaves underneath, closing the skin over them. The remaining basil is for garnish. Season well.

Grill the chicken for about 10 minutes on each side under a preheated moderate grill, or sauté in a little oil if you prefer. The cooking time will depend on the thickness of the chicken breast: test by inserting a fork or sharp knife into the meat to check it is cooked through and tender. If the juices run pink, cook for a little longer. Take care not to overcook or the meat fibres will become tough.

While the chicken is cooking, make the sauce: put the chives and cream into a saucepan and cook over a low heat for 6 minutes. Do not boil. Remove from the heat and stir in the basil. Season to taste.

When the chicken breasts are cooked, put them on to a warmed serving dish and pour over a little basil cream sauce. Garnish with the remaining basil. Serve the remaining sauce separately.

Cook's note: Basil cream sauce can be served with a variety of warm dishes, such as fresh salmon or trout, or escalopes of turkey, or served cold as a dressing poured over a green salad or a basil and tomato salad.

CHICKEN IN FRESH PEACH SAUCE

Our summer garden party is held on the first Sunday in July. It was originally held to celebrate our first six months in Burbage, and on that occasion smoked haddock and prawn terrine (see page 60) was on the menu. Now it has become an annual event. After our guests have left and everything has been put away, we carry our supper out to the scout-tent 'marquee'. This is a favourite post-party supper dish. Ripe, well-flavoured peaches are most important, as is the wine, which should be a Chardonnay.

SERVES 4

60g/2oz unsalted butter
90ml/3fl oz vegetable oil
4 boneless free-range chicken breasts, lightly dusted with plain flour
4 spring onions, white part only, finely chopped
300ml/10fl oz Australian Chardonnay
4 tablespoons clear honey
juice of 1 small lemon
salt and freshly ground black pepper
4 teaspoons cornflour, mixed with 120ml/4fl oz cold water
4 fresh, ripe peaches, skinned and stones removed
150ml/5fl oz double cream
chopped fresh parsley to garnish

Melt the butter with the oil in a large frying pan with a lid. Add the chicken breasts and brown them, turning often to seal well all over. Remove and set aside. Add the spring onion to the pan and sauté for about 1 minute, then pour in the Chardonnay, honey and lemon juice. Season well and stir. Return the chicken to the pan, cover, and simmer for 25 to 30 minutes until tender. If the liquid reduces too much, a little water can be added to the pan.

When the chicken is cooked, remove from the pan and keep warm. Add the slackened cornflour to the juices in the frying pan and cook for a couple of minutes until the liquid has thickened. Cut 3 of the peaches in half and put into a food processor. Pour in the pan juices and blend together until smooth.

Pour the peach sauce back into the pan and stir in the cream. Heat gently over a low heat; do not boil. Return the chicken to the pan and heat gently until warmed through. Turn out on to a warmed serving dish or dinner plates, and sprinkle with a little parsley. Slice the remaining peach, arrange the slices evenly around the chicken and serve.

CHICKEN WITH PRUNES AND BACON

Prunes, once the scourge of children in nurseries and school canteens, have taken on a new meaning with the introduction of Mediterranean and French dishes. We have realized that the sweetness of the prune sharpens the flavour of meat and complements fish without overwhelming it, making altogether richer-tasting dishes. If you have forgotten to soak the prunes overnight, just cover them with boiling water and they will not take long to soften. Reserve any liquid the prunes have been soaking in and add it to this dish or another – it is much too good to throw away. This dish can be prepared a day ahead and reheated when required. It can also be frozen.

SERVES 4

60g/2oz butter
90ml/3fl oz vegetable oil
8 rashers streaky bacon, rind removed, chopped
1 onion, peeled and finely chopped
4 boneless free-range chicken breasts
150ml/5fl oz chicken or vegetable stock
3 teaspoons cornflour, mixed with 90ml/3fl oz water
500g/1lb prunes, soaked in water overnight
30g/1oz blanched halved almonds
150ml/5fl oz single cream
salt and freshly ground black pepper

Melt the butter with the oil in a heavy-based frying pan. Add the bacon and onion, and cook until the onion is soft. Push the onion to one side of the pan and put in the chicken breasts. Raise the heat and sauté the chicken until sealed and well browned, then lower the heat and pour in the stock. Cover and simmer gently for 25 to 30 minutes.

When the chicken is tender and well cooked through, remove from the pan and keep warm. Add the slackened cornflour to the juices in the pan and mix well together. Bring to the boil and reduce the liquid a little, then lower the heat once more and add the prunes and almonds. Simmer for 10 minutes. Pour in the cream and heat through without boiling. Stir the liquid well and return the chicken to the pan. Baste with the sauce, season to taste and serve.

GINGER-SPICED CHICKEN WITH PINEAPPLE GINGER RICE

It was a really foul-weather evening. The wind was howling in the trees and the rain pouring down in torrents. Four friends were coming to dinner and, amazingly, they all arrived on time. But we had been prepared to wait, and had chosen a dish that doesn't mind waiting either. With its spices and ginger, it was a good dish for such a wild, cold evening. Making it will take a little time, but when the wonderful aromas start to fill the kitchen, and later when you sit down to enjoy the spicy flavour and creamy texture, you will realize it was worth it – a dish to get the tastebuds jumping.

SERVES 4 to 6

STAGE 1:
5cm/2-inch piece fresh root ginger, peeled and very thinly sliced
2 cloves garlic, crushed with a little salt
240ml/8fl oz cold water

STAGE 2:
240ml/8fl oz vegetable oil
8 boneless free-range chicken breasts, cut into small pieces
8 whole cloves
2 sticks cinnamon
seeds extracted from 8 cardamom pods
2 medium onions, peeled and finely chopped
300ml/10fl oz chicken stock
½ block creamed coconut
1 teaspoon ground coriander
2 teaspoons ground cumin
salt and freshly ground black pepper
90g/3oz whole almonds
150ml/5fl oz single cream

FOR THE PINEAPPLE GINGER RICE:
60g/2oz butter
1 medium onion, peeled and chopped
350g/12oz long-grain rice
300ml/10fl oz pineapple juice
450ml/15fl oz water
sea salt and freshly ground black pepper
2 whole pieces preserved ginger, finely chopped
4 spring onions, cut into small rings
freshly ground black pepper
250g/8oz fresh pineapple, cut into smallish pieces

Stage 1: liquidize the ingredients until smooth and creamy. Set aside until required.

Stage 2: heat the oil in a large frying pan. Add some of the chicken pieces and sauté quickly until slightly browned all over. Remove and repeat with the remaining chicken pieces. Set aside.

Put the cloves, cinnamon and cardamom seeds into the pan and fry for a few seconds to release the flavour, then remove them from the pan and wrap in a small piece of muslin. Tie the top firmly to make a bag, and set aside.

Add the onion to the pan and fry until golden-brown. A little more oil can be added if necessary. Pour in the creamy ginger mixture from stage 1 and cook for a couple of minutes. Pour in the stock and then add the creamed coconut, which melts down in cooking. Add the spice bag, coriander, cumin and seasonings, and then the chicken pieces, plus any juices that have drained from them. Simmer for around 45 minutes until the chicken is tender, stirring from time to time. If the sauce has not reduced and thickened as you like it, a little extra cooking time will do the job for you.

Meanwhile, pour boiling water on to the almonds and allow them to soak for about 4 minutes. Rub off the brown skins: they should come off quite easily after soaking. Lightly toast the almonds under a hot grill. Set aside until the chicken is cooked and the rice prepared. (Continued overleaf.)

To prepare the rice: melt the butter in a flameproof casserole, add the onion and cook until soft but not brown. Add the rice and sauté for a few minutes, stirring all the time. Pour in the pineapple juice and water and season to taste. Cover tightly, turn the heat right down and cook for 25 to 30 minutes. Ten minutes before the end of cooking time, put in the ginger and spring onion. When ready, mill over black pepper, and keep warm. A couple of minutes before serving, remove the lid and scatter the pineapple pieces around the top.

When the chicken is ready, remove the spice bag and discard, scatter in the toasted almonds, pour in the cream and stir well. Serve with the pineapple ginger rice.

CURRIED CHICKEN AND FRUIT SALAD

Although primarily a summer dish, this recipe – one of our favourites – can be adapted to use up leftover cooked turkey at Christmas: substitute fresh pears for peaches.

SERVES 4 to 6

6 cooked free-range chicken breasts, skin removed
150ml / 5fl oz whipping cream
4 teaspoons curry paste
120ml / 4fl oz fromage frais
2 large bananas
175g / 6oz seedless grapes
2 eating apples, peeled, cored and sliced
2 fresh ripe peaches, skinned, stoned and sliced
salt and freshly ground black pepper
crisp lettuce leaves and chopped fresh parsley to garnish
pineapple and mint jelly (page 262)

Cut the chicken into bite-sized pieces and set aside. Pour the cream into a large bowl, add the curry paste and whisk together until the cream just holds its shape. It should be of a coating consistency. Fold in the fromage frais.

Peel the bananas, cut the flesh into chunks, then fold into the curried cream mixture. If the grapes are large, cut them in half; add to the bananas in the curried cream. Fold in the slices of apple and peach. Put in the chicken pieces and mix well together. Season to taste. Arrange a border of fresh, crisp lettuce leaves on a serving dish, and pile the chicken mixture in the centre. Serve the jelly separately. Alternatively, chop the pineapple and mint jelly, arrange around the dish on top of the lettuce and pile in the chicken mixture as before. Sprinkle with parsley and serve.

TURKEY FILLET WITH CELERY
AND LOVAGE CREAM SAUCE

Fillets of turkey do not take very long to cook through, which is why they are so good for quick, last-minute dishes. Indeed, care must be taken not to over-cook them, or the meat fibres will toughen and become chewy. This recipe can be made with slices of chicken breast as well as turkey. The addition of the somewhat unusual herb lovage gives a piquancy to the creamy sauce. The dish can either be made in advance and kept warm, or cooked at the very last moment, depending on whether your guests take their drinks in the drawing room or, as is usual with us, come straight to the kitchen where you can cook and talk at the same time.

SERVES 4

60g/2oz unsalted butter
2 sticks celery, white part only, finely chopped
1 medium clove garlic, crushed with a little salt
2 shallots, finely chopped
4 tablespoons vegetable oil
500g/1lb turkey breast fillets, thinly sliced
150ml/5fl oz chicken stock
1 level tablespoon cornflour, mixed with 120ml/4fl oz water
1 sprig fresh lovage, finely snipped with scissors
120ml/4fl oz double cream
salt and freshly ground black pepper

Melt the butter in a deep frying pan and add the celery, garlic and shallot. Sauté for a few minutes until the celery and shallot are soft. Remove from the pan and set aside.

Put the vegetable oil into the frying pan, add the turkey fillets and seal over a high heat until nicely browned on both sides, taking care not to overcook. Remove the turkey from the pan and keep warm.

Return the celery, garlic and shallot mixture to the pan and pour in the stock. Simmer for a couple of minutes. Stir in the slackened cornflour and mix well until the sauce has thickened. Add the lovage, stir in the cream and season to taste. Turn the heat right down and return the turkey to the pan to finish cooking in the sauce for a few minutes.

You can keep the turkey warm in the pan on a very low heat until you need it. Alternatively, put the turkey and sauce into an ovenproof dish, cover with kitchen foil and keep warm in a low oven on the bottom shelf.

TURKEY AND BACON RISSOLES WITH TARRAGON SAUCE

We make these rissoles to use up Christmas turkey and bread sauce. Combined with ginger and lots of pepper they are spicy and tasty. Indeed they are so good that it is worth buying turkey fillets just to make them. Angela made a batch of two dozen one Christmas for guests arriving over the holiday, and they lasted an evening. They can be served as a main course accompanied by carrots, parsnips and potato cakes. For a simpler, lighter meal, serve with a fresh orange and green leaves salad, or a homemade coleslaw (page 136). If you make the rissoles smaller, they can be served with drinks, using the sauce as a dip.

SERVES 4 to 6

30g/1oz unsalted butter
1 small clove garlic, crushed with a little salt
1 medium onion, peeled and finely chopped
500g/1lb cooked turkey, minced
2 pieces preserved ginger, roughly chopped
3 level tablespoons cold bread sauce
1 tablespoon macadamia nuts or almonds, roughly chopped
1 teaspoon salt
freshly ground black pepper
8 to 12 rashers smoked streaky bacon (2 per rissole), rind removed

FOR THE SAUCE:
30g/1oz unsalted butter
1 medium onion, peeled and finely chopped
300ml/10fl oz chicken or turkey stock
1 teaspoon chopped tarragon, fresh or freeze-dried
3 teaspoons cornflour, mixed with 180ml/6fl oz milk
salt and freshly ground black pepper
150ml/5fl oz single cream

Preheat the oven to 190°C/375°F/gas 5.

Melt the butter in a frying pan over a low heat. Add the garlic and onion and cook until the onion is soft but not brown. Remove from the heat and allow to cool.

Put the turkey, ginger, bread sauce, nuts and salt into a mixing bowl. Give the pepper mill quite a number of turns over the mixture. Add the cooled onion and garlic and mix all the ingredients well together. Form into 4 large or 6 smaller rissoles and wrap each one with 2 rashers of bacon in the form of a cross. Place on a greased baking tray and cook in the preheated oven for 30 to 35 minutes until the bacon is crisp and golden. If smaller rissoles are made, 20 to 25 minutes' cooking time should suffice. Check the rissoles are cooked right through.

Meanwhile, make the sauce: melt the butter in a frying pan and add the onion. Cook until the onion is soft, then add the stock and tarragon and cook over a low heat for 10 minutes. Remove from the heat. Pour in the slackened cornflour, beating well to prevent any lumps forming. Return to the heat and cook for a further 5 minutes. Season to taste and add the cream. Heat gently but do not allow to boil. Serve the rissoles hot, with the sauce either poured over or handed separately in a warmed sauce boat.

SPICED TUDOR LAMB PATTIES
WITH PLUM AND BRANDY SAUCE

This recipe came about because a neighbour of ours rears his own free-range sheep and pigs. We bought a four-year-old sheep from him and experimented with delicious mutton dishes. We named this recipe Tudor Lamb because it was during the Tudor and Elizabethan age that fruit and spices were used in many meat dishes, mainly to cover up the strong smell of meat that was high due to the absence of refrigeration. (That is not the reason for putting spices into this particular recipe!) Mutton requires long, slow cooking, but is well worth the extra time it takes. These patties can be made from leftover cooked lamb or mutton and when served with a plum and brandy sauce make an excellent lunch or supper dish. They can be made well in advance, covered with clingfilm and put into the refrigerator (now that we have them!) until required.

SERVES 4

90ml/3fl oz olive or vegetable oil
1 eating apple, peeled, cored and finely chopped
1 onion, peeled and finely chopped
1.25kg/2½lb cooked lamb or mutton, minced
½ teaspoon ground allspice
3 large sprigs fresh rosemary, finely chopped
1 sprig fresh thyme, finely chopped
1 teaspoon ground ginger
2 tablespoons jellied meat stock
1 large free-range egg, beaten
salt and freshly ground black pepper
125g/4oz raisins
2 fresh figs, finely chopped (finely chopped prunes can be used if preferred)
a little extra oil for cooking the patties
1 recipe quantity plum and brandy sauce (page 250)

Heat the oil in a saucepan, add the apple and onion and cook gently until soft. Transfer the cooked apple and onion to a large bowl. Put the minced lamb or mutton into the bowl along with the allspice, herbs, ginger, jellied stock, egg and seasonings. Mix thoroughly together. Stir in the raisins and figs evenly.

Form the mixture into patties about 1cm/½ inch thick and 10 to 12cm/4 to 5 inches across. Cover and put into the refrigerator until required.

To serve: put a little oil into a frying pan and fry the patties on both sides until golden-brown. Serve with plum and brandy sauce.

Cook's note: The patties may feel a little damp when taken out of the refrigerator. This is fine, indeed it's better to keep them moist. They will become crisp on the outside when cooked, but should retain moistness inside.

LAMB'S LIVER IN LIME BUTTER SAUCE WITH SAFFRON MINT PILAF

Although calf's liver has the best flavour and is the tenderest of the livers, some prefer the fuller flavour of the dark liver from pasture-fed animals. Indeed, we favour the liver from these animals, because we do not agree with the way milk-fed calves are treated. Nor will you find on our menus foie gras, from force-fed geese and ducks, the price of which would be the same as the product itself: inflated, overrated, unnecessary and cruel. Please, if we possibly can, let us all buy meat from animals that have been compassionately farmed: free-range, with access to fresh air, green pasture and sunlight. If we cannot find this, let's complain to supermarkets, butchers and other food sellers until they stock only natural, properly reared, real food products. We need action, not just words.

SERVES 3 to 4

FOR THE SAFFRON MINT PILAF:
30g/1oz butter
1 small onion, peeled and finely chopped
150g/5oz long-grain rice
450ml/15fl oz chicken stock or water
salt and freshly ground black pepper
5 saffron strands, crushed
2 tablespoons chopped fresh mint
30g/1oz butter, cut into tiny pieces

FOR THE LIVER:
350g/12oz lamb's liver, trimmed and thinly sliced
1 tablespoon plain flour, seasoned with ½ teaspoon each of salt, dry
mustard, cayenne pepper and black pepper
90g/3oz unsalted butter
½ small clove garlic, crushed with a little salt
150ml/5fl oz sweet white wine (if you only have dry, add 3 teaspoons
clear honey to the sauce)
grated rind and juice of 1 lime

First make the pilaf: preheat the oven to 180°C/350°F/gas 4. Melt the butter in a large saucepan, put in the onion and cook until soft but not brown. Add the rice and cook for 4 minutes, stirring all the time, then pour in the stock or water and add the seasonings to taste and the saffron. Stir together well and bring to the boil. Pour the contents of the pan into an ovenproof dish, cover and cook in the preheated oven for 30 minutes until all the liquid is absorbed. Remove from the oven and keep warm until needed. Before serving, fork in the mint and butter.

To prepare the liver: dust the slices with the seasoned flour. Melt half the butter in a frying pan, add half the liver and sauté for 3 to 4 minutes on each side. Remove the cooked liver and add the remaining butter and liver slices. Sauté as before. Put the cooked liver into a serving dish and keep warm. Put the garlic, wine and lime rind and juice into the pan. Add honey if a dry wine is used. Bring to simmering point and continue to simmer until reduced by a third. Pour the sauce over the liver and serve with the prepared saffron mint pilaf.

SAUTÉED LAMB'S LIVER WITH RAISINS AND ORANGE SAUCE

During our outside catering days in the early 1970s, we would regularly cook and serve lunch for a wonderful old lady, the Hon. Mrs Duncan-Campbell. Although in her nineties, she still entertained and held lively lunch and drinks parties. She had had a lot of staff when younger, and was brought up in the old school of everyone knowing their place, especially in the below-stairs hierarchy. Since I served lunch and wine and saw to the guests as they arrived, I was placed on a level with the butler, and therefore all communication had to be through me. I was to pass on messages to Angela, the 'cook', even when we were in the kitchen together and all within earshot of each other. We often cooked this dish as a first course, as it was 'good for everybody'. Fresh orange and raisins turn liver into something a little more unusual and attractive. It is suitable as a first course, with the liver sliced finely into strips and served in small ramekins. It is also good for lunch or supper, served with creamed potatoes and an orange and green leaves salad.

SERVES 8 to 10 AS A STARTER, 4 AS A MAIN COURSE

125g/4oz raisins
grated rind and juice of 2 large oranges
350g/12oz lamb's liver, trimmed and thinly sliced
4 tablespoons plain flour, seasoned with salt and freshly ground black pepper
60g/2oz unsalted butter
4 tablespoons vegetable oil
1 small clove garlic, crushed with a little salt
juice of 1 lemon
150ml/5fl oz chicken stock
1 tablespoon redcurrant jelly
chopped fresh parsley to garnish

Put the raisins into a bowl and add the orange rind and juice. Set aside to allow the raisins to soak up the liquid and become plump.

Coat the slices of liver lightly in the seasoned flour. Melt half the butter with the oil in a sauté pan. Put in the liver and fry quickly on both sides to seal. Add the remaining butter halfway through frying. Remove the liver from the pan, put into an ovenproof dish and keep warm.

Put the garlic and the soaked raisins with their orange rind and juice into the pan. Add the lemon juice, stock and redcurrant jelly and simmer until the liquid is reduced by one third. Lower the heat and return the liver to the pan. Cover and simmer gently until the liver is just tender. Keep the heat low so that the liver is not overcooked and made tough. Should the sauce be a little too thick, pour in a little water to slacken it to the desired consistency.

When the liver is ready, sprinkle the parsley over it and serve.

LAMB ROAST WITH FRESH ORANGE AND HERB STUFFING

Grazing or meadow-fed lamb, which has had lush green pasture to graze on, and is not slaughtered until it is a year old, is the best for flavour and colour. Younger, milk-fed lamb, though the meat is tender, is lacking in flavour, and does not keep well. Eating older, grass-fed lamb is very much better for ewes, lambs and consumers alike. Friends of ours who have a smallholding in Herefordshire keep a herd of Ryland sheep. They are keeping alive a rare breed as well as producing their own mutton. When we are together we like to deplore the fact that mutton is no longer available from butcher's shops. We are favoured in receiving a share of our friends' mutton. Perhaps if we all lobbied our local butchers and supermarkets, someone, somewhere, might just listen, and we may once more be able to buy this delicious and economical meat as our foremothers used to do. We used a leg of mutton for this recipe for a Sunday lunch party and it was excellent, but lamb, if not too young, will be just as flavoursome when accompanied by the fruity, herb stuffing and red wine sauce. Use a good, fruit-flavoured Burgundy for the sauce.

SERVES 6 to 8

30g/1oz unsalted butter
1 large onion, peeled and finely chopped
90g/3oz wholemeal breadcrumbs
60g/2oz sultanas
60g/2oz raisins
½ teaspoon chopped fresh thyme
½ teaspoon chopped fresh rosemary
grated rind of 2 oranges
salt and freshly ground black pepper
juice of 1 orange
2kg/4½ lb boned leg of lamb

FOR THE GLAZE:
juice of ½ lemon
juice of 1 orange
60g/2oz light soft brown sugar or honey
120ml/4fl oz Worcestershire sauce

FOR THE SAUCE:
120ml/4fl oz red wine
300ml/10fl oz beef stock
orange segments and watercress to garnish

Preheat the oven to 190°C/375°F/gas 5.

Melt the butter in a frying pan and fry the onion for about 3 minutes. Put the breadcrumbs, dried fruit and fried onion into a bowl and mix together. Stir in the herbs and orange rind, season well and pour in the orange juice. Bind the stuffing together.

Wipe the leg of lamb with a clean, damp cloth, then pack the stuffing into it. Secure the joint with string and place in a greased roasting pan. Put all the glaze ingredients into a saucepan and bring to the boil, then pour over the meat. Roast the joint in the oven for 2 hours, basting often.

When cooked, remove the meat and keep warm on a serving dish. Pour the wine and stock into the roasting pan. Bring to the boil, scraping all the meat juices from the pan and mixing in well. Boil briskly until the liquid has reduced and thickened slightly. Season to taste.

Remove the string from the meat and serve garnished with orange segments and watercress, with the sauce handed separately in a warmed sauce boat.

PORK ESCALOPES WITH APPLE MUSTARD MAYONNAISE

Angela's great-aunt Iris Syrett used to cook this dish for family visits. It is served cold, so can be made in advance of guests arriving, leaving the host or hostess free to entertain. It is also a good dish for picnics, but cut the escalopes into fork-sized pieces for easy eating first.

SERVES 6

6 pork escalopes
90g/3oz unsalted butter
300ml/10fl oz mayonnaise
2 tablespoons Dijon mustard
250g/8oz thick apple purée (sweetened to taste)
salt and freshly ground black pepper
chopped fresh parsley and slices of apple (cut at the last minute) to garnish

Trim the pork escalopes, removing any excess fat. Melt the butter in a frying pan and sauté the escalopes for about 10 minutes on each side (the timing depends on the thickness of the escalopes). Take care not to overcook the meat or it will become tough, though it must be cooked through thoroughly. When the pork is tender and just turning golden-brown, remove from the pan and place on a board or plate to cool.

Put the mayonnaise into a mixing bowl, add the mustard and the apple purée, season to taste, and blend well together.

Arrange the cold pork escalopes on a long serving dish and spoon over the apple and mustard mayonnaise until all the meat is well coated with sauce. Put into the refrigerator until required. Just before serving, sprinkle the parsley over and arrange the sliced apple around the meat. Serve with a fresh green salad.

TENDERLOIN OF PORK WITH MANGO AND APPLE SAUCE

This dish appears regularly on our restaurant menu because it is fairly quick to prepare and can be made to order. It is excellent for unexpected guests or when numbers are greater than the original booking. It also helps to sell a few bottles of Chablis, its perfect accompaniment. Reducing the liquid for the sauce is very important. If it is not properly reduced and thickened, its consistency will be loose, and the texture and flavour will be affected.

SERVES 4

30g/1oz butter
4 tablespoons vegetable oil
2 small pork tenderloins, sliced and beaten into 8 escalopes
(you can buy them ready prepared if preferred)
2 good-flavoured eating apples, peeled, cored and sliced
120ml/4fl oz wine such as Chablis
(the remaining wine can accompany the meal)
150ml/5fl oz chicken stock
juice of ½ lemon
2 tablespoons mango chutney
sea salt and freshly ground black pepper
120ml/4fl oz double cream
chopped fresh parsley to garnish

Melt the butter with the oil in a frying pan, put in the escalopes 2 at a time and lightly brown the meat on both sides. When all 8 escalopes are cooked, put into a dish and keep warm. Put the apple slices into the pan and sauté for a couple of minutes. Pour in the wine and stock and simmer until the liquid has reduced by half, then add the lemon juice, chutney, salt and plenty of pepper. Simmer to blend for a couple of minutes. Add the cream and stir in well. Do not boil. Pour the sauce over the pork escalopes, sprinkle a little parsley over and serve.

TENDERLOIN OF PORK WITH LEMON AND MUSHROOM SAUCE

Our friends who have a farm in Herefordshire keep a Gloucester Old Spot pig. A couple of years ago she had a litter of a dozen piggies. They would run all over the farm and even down the lane into the neighbouring field, but at feeding time Frank would whistle loudly and all twelve would come running from wherever they were. They were nicknamed the hooligans and not without cause. These were the free-est free-range piglets we have come across, and rightly so.

SERVES 4 to 6

2 pork tenderloins
1 tablespoon seasoned plain flour

FOR THE SAUCE:
125g/4oz unsalted butter
175g/6oz field or cultivated mushrooms, thinly sliced
60g/2oz plain flour
600ml/1 pint milk
2 teaspoons chopped fresh herbs (such as parsley, chives, thyme)
*finely grated rind and juice of 2 lemons (a nutmeg grater will grate the
rind finely enough for it to blend well into the sauce)*
1 level tablespoon caster sugar
salt and freshly ground black pepper
150ml/5fl oz vegetable oil
chopped fresh parsley to garnish

Cut the pork into 2.5cm/1-inch pieces, removing any white skin. Place the pieces of pork cut-side down between 2 pieces of strong clingfilm and flatten the meat gently with a rolling pin. Remove the clingfilm and dust the meat with seasoned flour.

Make the sauce: melt half the butter in a pan, add the mushrooms and cook over a low heat, stirring all the time, until they change colour and the juices begin to run. Remove the mushrooms and set aside. Put the remaining butter into the pan and when it has melted add the flour and cook for 2 minutes. Pour in the milk a little at a time, beating well. Add the herbs, lemon rind and juice, sugar, and the cooked mushrooms. Season well to taste. Simmer slowly while the pork is being cooked.

Put the oil into a frying pan. Add the pork pieces, a few at a time, and sauté for 2 to 3 minutes on each side. Remove the cooked pork as you go and keep warm. If the pork has been beaten very thinly, the cooking will not take long. When all the pork has been cooked, put on to a warmed serving dish, pour the sauce over, sprinkle with parsley and serve.

BACON AND HERB-STUFFED PORK TENDERLOIN

Many years ago Angela and I were invited to dinner by friends who were of a frame of mind more literary than domestic, and with whom dinner was usually a hit-or-miss affair. This particular evening was no exception. The main course was pork in some sort of sauce and I soon found out that it was a 'boil in the bag' dinner, and that it was still in its bag. About a quarter of the way through my dinner I had discreetly to remove a piece of thick polythene from my mouth. My neighbour had the other half of the bag. Neither of us said a word, just quietly pushed our halves of the 'bag' under some vegetables at the side of our plates. This recipe will not be found 'boiled in a bag'.

SERVES 4 to 6

30g/1oz unsalted butter
1 small onion, peeled and finely chopped
5 rashers smoked streaky bacon, rind removed
90g/3oz fresh wholemeal breadcrumbs
grated rind of 1 small lemon
small bunch fresh thyme, chopped
small bunch chives, chopped
1 small free-range egg
salt and freshly ground black pepper
2 pork tenderloins, trimmed; flattened between clingfilm with a rolling pin
chopped fresh parsley to garnish

FOR THE GRAVY:
2 teaspoons cornflour, mixed with 4 tablespoons water
1 teaspoon chopped fresh tarragon
1 teaspoon Dijon mustard
120ml/4fl oz double cream

Gently melt the butter in a saucepan, then add the onion and cook until soft. Chop 3 of the bacon rashers into small pieces and add them to the onion. Cook together for about 4 minutes.

Put the sautéed onion and bacon, the breadcrumbs, lemon rind, thyme, chives, egg and seasonings into a mixing bowl. Bind together.

Preheat the oven to 160°C/325°F/gas 3. Take the pieces of flattened tenderloin and lay stuffing mixture down the centre of each. Season again to taste and roll up into a sausage shape. Tuck in the ends to keep the stuffing in. Tie with string or secure with a skewer if you wish. Put the tenderloins into an ovenproof dish and lay a rasher of the remaining bacon the full length of each one. Bake in the preheated oven for 1 hour until the meat is tender.

To make the gravy: pour the juices from the cooked meat into a saucepan. Add the slackened cornflour and stir well until thickened. Stir in the tarragon, mustard and cream. Slice the tenderloin into slices, not too thin or the stuffing will fall out. Arrange on a warmed serving dish or dinner plates. Serve with the gravy poured over and parsley sprinkled on top.

DRAMBUIE DUCK WITH ORANGE SAUCE

Mrs Beeton tells us in her book of *Household Management* that it is during the green-pea season that duck is usually found on the English table, peas being the traditional accompaniment to roast duck, even though November is the proper duck season. These days duck seems to be in butcher's shops and supermarkets all year round, green-pea season or not. In this recipe the duck meat is sautéed to seal in the juices then baked in the oven with the sauce. Leave the dish uncovered in the latter stages of cooking: this will give the duck a lovely crispy skin. Quite a straightforward dish to prepare, it is ideal for a lunch or dinner party, or can even be adapted as a celebration meal for two, when with correct presentation it will be like 'eating out at home'.

SERVES 8

60g/2oz unsalted butter
120ml/4fl oz vegetable oil
8 boneless duck breasts
2 onions, peeled and finely chopped
1 clove garlic, crushed with a little salt
120ml/4fl oz balsamic vinegar
90g/3oz acacia honey
300ml/10fl oz game stock, or 1 beef stock cube in 300ml/10fl oz boiling water
grated rind and juice of 2 medium oranges
juice of ½ lemon
240ml/8fl oz Drambuie
2 tablespoons cornflour, mixed with 180ml/6fl oz cold water
salt and freshly ground black pepper

Preheat the oven to 180°C/350°F/gas 4.

Melt the butter with the oil in a sauté pan. Put in the duck breasts and seal until brown on both sides. Remove the duck from the pan and set aside.

Put the onion and garlic into the pan and cook until the onion is soft. Add the vinegar and honey and simmer until the mixture becomes syrupy. Pour in the stock, the orange rind and the orange and lemon juices and simmer for a further 5 minutes. Pour in the Drambuie and the slackened cornflour, stir and cook until the sauce thickens. Season to taste.

Put the duck breasts, skin-side up, into an ovenproof dish and pour the sauce over. Cook in the preheated oven for 20 to 25 minutes. The timing will depend upon the thickness of the duck breasts; if they are small and thin, test after 15 minutes.

When the duck is cooked, remove from the oven, slice thinly and place on a warmed serving dish or dinner plates. Serve with a fresh orange and green leaf salad.

WILD DUCK WITH APRICOTS

This dish reminds us of a lunch we cooked for a party of film actors, actresses and their families in Gloucestershire a few years ago. Among the guests were an Italian prince and the ex-wife of Sean Connery. The guests were entering the dining room and seating themselves but I couldn't find Angela anywhere. At last I located a small voice coming from behind the heavy oak loo door, and watched as the brass doorknob rotated round and round but the door remained firmly closed. I tried from the outside but the latch would not spring back. I returned to the dining room to serve the wine and pass round the bread, then rushed back to the loo door. We both held the knob and gave it a good hard turn. Success. The door latch yielded and out bounded Angela. I shudder to think what would have happened if she had not got out of that predicament. However, the lunch went off well, and as we were leaving we passed the loo door and noticed the brass door knob rotating slowly round and round. I wonder who it was?

SERVES 4

2 wild duck
2 good sprigs fresh thyme
sea salt and freshly ground black pepper
600ml/1 pint apple juice
60g/2oz butter, softened
250g/8oz fresh apricots, skinned and stones removed
liqueur-glass Cointreau
150ml/5fl oz double cream or crème fraîche

Preheat the oven to 230°C/450°F/gas 8.
    Wash the ducks under cold running water inside and out, then dry with absorbent paper. Place in a roasting pan. Push a sprig of thyme into the cavity of each duck. Rub a little salt into the skin and grind some pepper over. Pour half the apple juice over the

birds and smear with the butter. Roast in the preheated oven for 20 minutes. (This produces rare meat. You can cook a little longer, but no more than 30 minutes or the duck could become grey and dry.)

While the ducks are roasting, cook the apricots in the remaining apple juice until soft. Put into a food processor, pour in the Cointreau and liquidize. Pour the sauce into a saucepan.

Remove the ducks from the oven and place on a carving board. Cut each in half, or carve from the whole birds if you prefer. Pour the meat juices from the roasting pan into the sauce, stir in the cream or crème fraîche and warm through gently. Pour the sauce over the duck and serve.

DUCK AND BACON SAUSAGES WITH WHISKY AND ORANGE SAUCE

We were once asked during our outside catering days to do a lunch for the local Silver Threads senior citizens' group. We understood it to be a buffet for 180. Arriving at the village hall loaded with plates, boxes and food, we were very nervous to see tables set up and laid with cutlery. We were told that it was no longer a buffet but a sit-down affair because the senior citizens did not want to be up and down during lunch. We are still not sure how the two of us managed to prepare, cook and serve all those people. It wasn't until the very end of the meal, when the diners actually applauded us, that we came out of automatic-pilot mode. These sausages will always remind us of that amazing lunch. The duck fat is essential to this recipe because it helps to bind the ingredients and also enhances the flavour. If the sauce is too sharp for your taste, add a little sugar or clear honey when putting in the cooked orange and lemon rind.

SERVES 4

500g/1lb duck breast, minced (a good butcher will do this for you if you do not have a mincer)
4 rashers smoked streaky bacon, rind removed, minced or chopped very finely
250g/8oz sausagemeat
60g/2oz fresh white breadcrumbs
4 sage leaves, chopped
1 teaspoon ground ginger
½ teaspoon cayenne pepper
salt and freshly ground black pepper
sausage skins, if desired
a little plain flour for dusting the skinless sausages
oil for frying

FOR THE SAUCE:
2 oranges
1 lemon
600ml / 1 pint boiling water
1 grapefruit
3 tablespoons orange marmalade or redcurrant jelly
180ml / 6fl oz whisky
2 heaped teaspoons arrowroot, mixed to a paste with a little water

Put the duck, bacon, sausagemeat, breadcrumbs, sage, ginger, cayenne pepper and seasonings into a mixing bowl and blend thoroughly together. If using sausage skins, fill them up. If not, form into sausage shapes, dust with the flour and chill for a couple of hours before frying.

To make the sauce: take the oranges and lemon and thinly peel away the rind without the pith. Cut the rind into very fine shreds. Put the shredded rind into the boiling water and boil for around 3 minutes. Drain off the water and set aside.

Squeeze the juice of the oranges, lemon and grapefruit into a saucepan, add the marmalade or redcurrant jelly, bring to the boil and simmer for 5 minutes. Pour in the whisky and remove from the heat.

Heat the oil for the sausages in a frying pan, add the sausages and fry, turning frequently, until golden-brown all over. Keep warm in a low oven while you finish the sauce: stir in the arrowroot paste and return the sauce to the heat. Cook briefly until it has thickened, stirring constantly. Put in the shredded citrus peel, stir well and serve with the fried sausages.

HEDGEROW PHEASANT CASSEROLE

When we were running the restaurant at Rockley Chapel, I would play the oboe on Sunday mornings after seeing that everything was ready for lunch. As I played I would be accompanied by a pheasant noisily defending the chapel porch as his territory. He would stop as soon as I stopped playing, then start as soon as I began again. This recipe is dedicated to Rockley's courageous pheasant. The sloe gin and juniper berries give this casserole a wonderful depth of colour and flavour. This is good for a dinner party as it can be prepared in advance and kept hot in the oven while you take a leisurely aperitif with your guests. Duchesse potatoes (page 171) are a good accompaniment: not only do they look good, they also mop up the casserole juices. This casserole can be frozen after it is cooked, or kept for a couple of days in the refrigerator: it improves with keeping.

SERVES 6 to 8

1 brace of pheasant, plucked and drawn ready for the oven
90g/3oz dripping or 240ml/8fl oz vegetable oil
plain flour seasoned with salt and pepper
90g/3oz smoked streaky bacon, rind removed, finely chopped
1 tablespoon plain flour
850ml/1½ pints beef or chicken stock
150ml/5fl oz sloe gin
4 sticks celery, chopped
4 eating apples such as Coxes, peeled, cored and chopped
grated rind and juice of 1 small lemon
15 juniper berries, crushed
½ teaspoon coriander seeds, crushed
sprig fresh rosemary, chopped
1 bay leaf
3 teaspoons Dijon mustard
3 level tablespoons redcurrant jelly
salt and freshly ground black pepper

Wash the prepared pheasants under cold running water inside and out until the water runs clear. Dry the pheasants with absorbent paper and trim away any loose pieces of skin, feathers and lumps of yellow fat. Any hairs can be burnt off over a gas flame, a lighter or a candle – take care not to drip candle wax on to the bird.

Preheat the oven to 190°C/375°F/gas 5.

Heat the dripping or oil until very hot in a large frying pan or roasting pan. Roll the pheasants in the seasoned flour and place in the pan. Sauté the birds all over until golden-brown. (This is important: browning the birds well adds greatly to their flavour.) When well browned, transfer the pheasants to a large casserole dish. Put the bacon into the pan and fry until just turning brown, then transfer to the dish with the pheasant. Stir the tablespoon of flour into the fat remaining in the pan to make a roux. Blend and cook the flour for a few minutes. Pour in the stock and sloe gin, stir well, then add all the remaining ingredients. Season well and bring to simmering point. Pour the sauce over the pheasants, cover and cook in the preheated oven for 3 hours. The cooking time will depend on the age of the pheasants; older birds will take longer to cook than young ones.

When the pheasants are well cooked, lift them out of the casserole and place on a wooden carving board. Skim off any fat that may be floating on top of the sauce. Joint the pheasants, removing any bones that are loose and unsightly. Return the pheasant to the casserole, cover and keep warm until required.

Cook's note: You can liquidize the sauce (no bones) for a smoother texture if desired.

PIGEON, BLACKBERRY AND APPLE CASSEROLE

The husband of an acquaintance of ours made a similar casserole to this one while learning to cook. The recipe required '3 sprigs thyme' and 'a couple of sprigs parsley'. He promptly removed the leaves from the thyme and parsley, threw them away and cooked the remaining bare sprigs! This is a good dish to cook when you are busy doing something else because it needs so little attention. And, once complete, it will happily sit in the oven keeping warm while you have a drink and relax with your guests. Wild rice is a good accompaniment and this also can be cooked in advance. Drain the cooked rice, dot with knobs of butter, cover with kitchen foil and keep warm in the oven. If you cannot get any sweet apple juice or a sweet cider and you use dry instead, add a little honey after the juices have thickened. This casserole can also be cooked in a slow cooker.

SERVES 4

60g/2oz unsalted butter
4 tablespoons vegetable oil
12 pigeon breasts
4 well-flavoured eating apples, peeled, cored and sliced
6 shallots, peeled and finely chopped
2 sprigs fresh thyme, leaves only
sea salt and freshly ground black pepper
150ml/5fl oz chicken stock
300ml/10fl oz sweet apple juice or sweet cider
120ml/4fl oz rich tawny port
1 tablespoon cornflour, mixed with 90ml/3fl oz cold water
grated rind and juice of ½ lemon
¼ teaspoon ground allspice
250g/8oz blackberries, washed

Preheat the oven to 140°C/275°F/gas 1.

Melt the butter with the oil in a large frying pan, then put in the pigeon breasts 2 at a time to seal. Cook on both sides until brown in colour, then remove and set aside. Lightly brown the apple slices in the pan, then set these aside also. Put the shallot into the pan and lightly brown, adding a little more oil if necessary. Lay half the apple and shallot in the bottom of an ovenproof dish. Put in the pigeon breasts, sprinkle the thyme leaves over and season well to taste. Lay the remaining apple and shallot over the pigeon. Pour in the stock and apple juice or cider, cover and cook in the preheated oven for 3½ hours.

When the pigeon is cooked, remove the dish from the oven and pour off the cooking juices into a saucepan. Pour in the port, and stir in the slackened cornflour, lemon rind and juice and allspice, and bring all to the boil, stirring constantly until the liquid thickens. When thickened, add the blackberries and blend in. Pour the sauce over the pigeon in the dish and serve.

RABBIT AND CIDER CASSEROLE

'It will never sell,' said Angela after being persuaded to buy some local rabbit by our game butcher. 'Just let's try it,' I replied. And so, with reservations, Angela made this casserole. Besides the rabbit the main ingredient is Somerset cider brandy, which is enhanced by the apple. When all are simmered together and the rabbit juices blend with the apple and cider brandy, it makes a wonderful caramelly stock. If you do not have the time to make the apple marmalade, redcurrant or crab apple jelly can be substituted. Calvados or brandy can also be substituted if you cannot get any cider brandy. Alternatively, omit the brandy altogether and make the cider up to 600ml/1 pint. We sold out completely the first evening this dish was on the menu, to our great surprise. Next morning Angela went out and bought lots more rabbit. Rabbit does tend to become dry in cooking, but sealing the meat first and then casseroling it keeps it lovely and moist. Serve with creamed potatoes to mop up the juices, or new potatoes and a chunk of homemade wholemeal bread which will absorb the gravy just as well.

SERVES 4 to 6

2 rabbits, skinned and jointed (your butcher will do this)
60g/2oz plain flour
1 teaspoon dry mustard
1 teaspoon salt
½ teaspoon cayenne pepper
freshly ground black pepper
180ml/6fl oz vegetable or olive oil for sealing the rabbit
2 medium onions, peeled and chopped
1 clove garlic, crushed with a little salt
6 ripe and well-flavoured eating apples, peeled, cored and sliced
450ml/15fl oz cider
150ml/5fl oz Somerset cider brandy

300ml / 10 fl oz chicken or game stock
3 tablespoons apple marmalade (page 264) or redcurrant
or crab apple jelly
1 bay leaf
a couple of sprigs fresh thyme
chopped fresh parsley to garnish

Wash the rabbit under cold running water, then dab dry with absorbent paper. Put the flour, mustard, salt and cayenne and black pepper into a bowl and mix together until the flour is well seasoned all through. Coat the rabbit meat with the seasoned flour. Pour the oil into a large flameproof casserole and brown the rabbit meat a little at a time over a medium heat. You may need to add more oil from time to time.

Set the browned rabbit aside and put the onion and garlic into the casserole. Cook for a couple of minutes. Add the apple and stir round the pan for a couple more minutes. Pour in the cider, cider brandy and stock and stir well. Stir in the apple marmalade or your chosen jelly, and pop in the bay leaf and sprigs of thyme. Return the rabbit to the casserole, season well to taste, cover with the lid and simmer over a low heat for at least 2 hours. The cooking time will depend upon the quality of the rabbit. The older it is, the longer it takes to cook. When the meat comes away from the bone easily, it is ready.

Remove and discard the bay leaf and sprigs of thyme. If you like a thicker sauce, remove the rabbit meat from the casserole and keep warm. Bring the sauce to the boil and cook until the liquid has reduced and thickened to your liking. Check the seasonings, put the rabbit back into the casserole, sprinkle parsley over and serve.

SWEET AND SOUR RABBIT

Monday is officially our day off but frequently finds Angela in the kitchen experimenting with a new recipe or trying out various combinations of flavours. This is one such Monday recipe. We both felt like having a Chinese-style dish and went through all the normal ingredients before coming up with this variation on a theme using rabbit instead of pork or prawns. I enjoyed this dish with its piquant, fruity flavours, and the absence of bones is bliss. Chinese plum sauce is available from good supermarkets. Boneless rabbit can be bought from most good supermarkets and butchers. Since rabbit meat is not very fatty and since there is no batter coating, this meal is healthier than the (westernized) version you get in a Chinese takeaway. Serve with a tossed green salad and/or basmati rice cooked in chicken stock.

SERVES 4

FOR THE MEATBALLS:
500g/1lb rabbit meat, minced
3 sprigs fresh thyme, finely chopped
1 clove garlic, crushed with a little sea salt
1 level tablespoon plain flour
60g/2oz fresh white breadcrumbs
¼ teaspoon ground mace
sea salt and freshly ground black pepper
1 small free-range egg, beaten

a little oil for frying the meatballs
chopped fresh parsley to garnish

FOR THE SAUCE:

60g/2oz demerara sugar
120ml/4fl oz balsamic vinegar
90ml/3fl oz soy sauce
60ml/2fl oz plum sauce
300ml/10fl oz pineapple or apple juice
2 tablespoons clear honey
juice of ½ lemon
2 tablespoons cornflour, mixed with 180ml/6fl oz cold water

First make the meatballs: put all the ingredients except the egg into a large mixing bowl. Mix well then add the egg and bind together. Form into walnut-size meatballs.

Then make the sauce: put the sugar, vinegar, soy sauce, plum sauce, pineapple or apple juice, honey and lemon juice into a heavy-based saucepan. Heat gently to dissolve the sugar. Pour in the slackened cornflour and bring to simmering point. Keep the sauce warm while cooking the meatballs.

Heat the oil in a frying pan and put in the meatballs. Shallow-fry, turning frequently, until they are golden-brown. When cooked, put them into a heatproof dish and keep warm in a low oven until required. Do not cover the meatballs once they are in the oven or they may loose their crispness. Once the sauce has heated through, remove the meatballs from the oven, pour the sauce over, sprinkle with parsley and serve.

VENISON AND BEEF STEAK SUET CRUST PUDDING

This suet pudding is an adaptation of an old English recipe but uses venison instead of the usual kidney. To serve you can turn the pudding out on to a serving dish and pour the gravy round it, or, more traditionally, you can wrap a white napkin around the outside of the basin and serve the pudding straight from it. The pudding is prepared in two stages over two days: the suet crust must be made on the day the pudding is required because it needs to be fresh and moist. The usual comment from our guests is that it is the best suet pudding they have ever eaten. Your patience in preparing it will be well rewarded.

SERVES 4 to 6

60g/2oz dripping
2 onions, peeled and chopped
1 clove garlic, crushed with a little salt
1 bay leaf
350g/12oz stewing venison, cut into cubes
350g/12oz lean stewing beef, cut into cubes
850ml/1½ pints beef stock
salt and freshly ground black pepper
90ml/3fl oz port

FOR THE SUET PASTRY:
butter for greasing the dish
250g/8oz self-raising flour
¼ teaspoon salt
¼ teaspoon freshly ground white pepper
1 teaspoon finely chopped fresh tarragon, or ½ teaspoon freeze-dried
125g/4oz beef or vegetable suet
120ml/4fl oz milk

The day before the pudding is to be served, melt the dripping in a large saucepan. Put in the onion and cook until soft. Add the garlic, bay leaf, venison and beef and stir for a few minutes before pouring in the stock. Season well, cover and bring to the boil, then turn down the heat and simmer gently for 3 hours until the meat is tender. Remove the meat from the gravy and keep the meat and the gravy separately until required.

The next day, grease an 850ml/1½-pint basin with butter. Cut out a circle of greaseproof paper to fit the bottom and place it in the basin. Make the suet pastry: put the flour, salt, pepper, tarragon and suet in a large mixing bowl and mix well together. Pour in the milk and stir to form a dough. If the mixture is too dry add a little more milk or water. The dough should be firm enough to roll out without sticking.

Separate about one-third of the pastry to form a lid and set aside. Roll out the remaining pastry into a circle. Cut a 'V' shape out of the circle (this makes it easier to fit the basin) and line the basin with the pastry dough, pressing the edges together firmly to prevent seepage. Fill the lined basin with the meat, then roll out a circle of dough for the lid and place this on top. Press the edges of the dough together. Cover the top with kitchen foil, scrunching the edge to secure firmly around the basin. Do not make the top too tight as this will prevent the pudding from rising. Steam for 1½ hours.

When the pudding is almost ready, pour the gravy into a saucepan, add the port and heat through. Turn out the steamed pudding or wrap the napkin around the basin and serve with the gravy handed separately in a warmed sauce-boat.

VENISON WITH CLARET AND REDCURRANT SAUCE

It was mid-winter and snowing hard when we arrived at a country house in the Cotswolds to cater for a fortieth-birthday celebration. There were to be forty guests and dinner was to be held in the old coach house across a cobbled courtyard. Being some way from the main house, this posed a problem for us. The first course was chilled crab soufflé, and was manageable. The main course, however, was this venison dish. Angela put the plates into the Aga to get as hot as possible. Taking twenty plates at a time, I sprinted over the courtyard as fast as the cobbles allowed, slowing down to a more dignified approach on reaching the table. Back in the kitchen Angela had arranged the venison on two large serving dishes. It was now snowing quite heavily and wet underfoot. Covering the dishes with kitchen foil, we both sprinted (as best we could) over the courtyard with dishes in hand. Angela went back for the vegetables, which were served in huge Victorian tureens, leaving me to serve the venison. We should have named this dish 'Sprinting Venison' to commemorate the occasion. Oh, yes – the pudding was dark chocolate orange cream gâteau with whipped brandy cream, served cold. Serve the venison with game chips or peppered creamed potatoes, Brussels sprouts and buttered carrots.

SERVES 4

60g/2oz unsalted butter
4 venison steaks
large wine-glass good fruity claret
2 tablespoons redcurrant jelly
2 tablespoons jellied meat stock
salt and freshly ground black pepper

Melt the butter in a heavy-based saucepan and fry the venison steaks according to taste, taking care not to overcook them. Remove from the pan and keep warm.

Deglaze the pan with the claret and mix well with the meat juices in the pan. Add the redcurrant jelly and jellied stock and season well. Cook until reduced to a syrupy sauce, stirring all the time. Put the venison on to a warmed serving dish, pour the sauce over and serve.

PEPPERED BRANDIED VENISON

This dish will always remind me of the outside-catering lunches we used to do for our marvellously energetic 90-year-old friend, the Hon. Mrs Duncan-Campbell. A visiting lord, whose name I forget, was a guest at one of her lunch parties. He drove a silver-coloured Rolls Royce, a beautiful motor but one which filled the driveway and prevented the gardener from getting his car out to go to his lunch. I was asked by the hostess, who was used to servants moving cars, to drive the car out of the way. I am only five foot tall, and this defect hadn't escaped the owner of the Rolls, who said I was not tall enough to move his car. Mrs Duncan-Campbell told him in no uncertain terms not to be 'such a silly arse'. Reluctantly he gave me the keys. Even though I could only look through the steering wheel and could barely get a toe on to the accelerator, I did manage to move the car forwards and out of the way. I could not reverse it, however, because if I turned my body to look out of the back window my toe would come off the accelerator, so the car stayed where it was, just outside the gate. This is the real reason I drive a Metro. This recipe is very easy to prepare, and is ideal for last-minute cooking or for unexpected guests. Fillet of venison must not be overcooked, but once prepared can be left in a warm (not too hot) oven until required. Creamed or sautéed potatoes are a good accompaniment, along with butter-tossed carrots and baked skinned tomatoes.

SERVES 4

500g/1lb venison fillet, sliced
1 tablespoon black peppercorns, crushed
60g/2oz unsalted butter
90ml/3fl oz vegetable oil
1 clove garlic, crushed with a little salt
150ml/5fl oz brandy
½ chicken stock cube, mixed with 90ml/3fl oz boiling water
1 level tablespoon cornflour, mixed with 150ml/5fl oz cold water
pinch of salt and freshly ground black pepper
120ml/4fl oz single cream
small handful chopped fresh chives
1 teaspoon caster sugar

Trim off any fat from the slices of venison and toss the meat in the crushed peppercorns.

Melt the butter with the oil in a large frying pan and add the garlic. Take a third of the meat and seal it quickly in the fat. Remove from the pan as soon as it is sealed and repeat the sealing process with the remainder of the meat, one third at a time. Fillet of venison must not be overcooked because it tends to become dry and the meat fibres to spoil. When all the meat has been sealed, return it to the pan and add the brandy. Stir in the stock, then add the slackened cornflour, stirring well to get rid of any lumps. Season well, pour in the cream and stir in the chives and sugar. The dish must not be allowed to boil at this stage. Check the seasonings and keep warm until ready to serve.

VENISON BURGERS
WITH RED CHERRY SAUCE

It was supposed to be summer and holiday time. We had rented a cottage on the South Devon coast overlooking a shingle shore and the sea. Our three dogs were asleep by the fire (yes, a fire in August – well, it is Britain). Deep grey-green waves with pure white crests crashed and foamed upon the stony beach, and it rained. It rained for the whole five days of our holiday. Just for a change we went shopping at the local supermarket. It was quite a good supermarket as it turned out, and among other items we found a fillet of fresh venison. I bought a bottle (several bottles actually) of Fleurie, Angela bought her favourite fruit, which is cherries, and we combined the two. We had half the venison roasted, and then turned the other half into burgers. The red cherry sauce enhances venison and gives a really good flavour, and rich, fruity Fleurie complements the meal perfectly. That is about all we can remember of that holiday except for our car breaking down at least four times. We were very pleased to be home and back at work for a rest.

SERVES 4

FOR THE BURGERS:
500g/1lb venison, finely minced
250g/8oz smoked streaky bacon, rind removed, minced
125g/4oz sausagemeat
4 tablespoons wholemeal breadcrumbs
salt and freshly ground black pepper
1 teaspoon cayenne pepper
1 clove garlic, crushed with a little salt
1 onion, peeled and finely chopped
2 teaspoons chopped fresh thyme

olive or vegetable oil to fry the burgers

FOR THE SAUCE:
175g/6oz dark red cherries, stones removed
2 cloves
300ml/10fl oz fresh orange juice
juice of ½ lemon
90ml/3fl oz ruby or tawny port
60g/2oz soft light brown sugar
1 teaspoon cornflour, mixed with a little water
30g/1oz butter

Put all the burger ingredients into a large mixing bowl and mix
well together. This can be done in a food processor if you wish.
Turn out the mixture and form into 8 even balls, then flatten into
burgers.

Then make the sauce: put the cherries, cloves and orange and
lemon juice into a saucepan and simmer for 10 minutes. Remove
and discard the cloves. Add the port, sugar and slackened
cornflour. Cook until the liquid begins to thicken. Add the butter
and stir thoroughly: this makes the sauce shiny.

Fry the venison burgers, pour over the hot sauce and serve.

5

Vegetarian and Salad Dishes

SPINACH, DATE, CHICORY AND ALMOND SALAD

Salads form a large part of our diet, especially for quick lunches when we are working in the restaurant. A substantial salad such as this one can be served as a meal by itself, with or without a chunk of homemade bread, or it can accompany a variety of dishes, meat or fish, and particularly vegetarian meals. We have served this salad as a refreshing first course before a rich main dish. It is particularly good for anyone watching their weight.

SERVES 4

20 almonds
¼ iceberg lettuce, very thinly sliced
1 head of chicory, cored and thinly sliced
10 fresh spinach leaves, thinly sliced
10 dates, stoned and finely chopped
freshly ground black pepper

FOR THE DRESSING:
1 tablespoon clear honey
120ml / 4fl oz white wine vinegar
240ml / 8fl oz grapeseed oil or light olive oil
a squeeze of lemon juice (about 1 teaspoon)
¼ clove garlic, crushed with a little salt

First make the dressing: put all the ingredients into a screw-topped jar and shake until they are well blended.

Soak the almonds in boiling water for 2 minutes, then rub them to remove the skins. Slice the almonds as thinly as you can.

Put all the salad ingredients, including the sliced almonds, into a bowl, pour over the dressing and toss a few times. Serve at once.

CRUNCHY COLESLAW

We are fortunate enough to have the original Victorian Kitchen Garden nearby at Chilton Manor, where head gardener Harry Dodson grows wonderful fruit and vegetables. The vegetables are just as they should be, firm, a good colour and full of flavour, bursting with memories of those days when food tasted like itself, wholesome and full of goodness. You would have to go a long way to find fresh produce as properly tended and carefully treated as these vegetables obviously are, and not a chemical or pesticide in sight. We are blessed indeed to be able to purchase our vegetables from such a delightful place. This coleslaw is a marvellous accompaniment to almost any meal. We very often have a plate of it just by itself, as it is very filling and nutritious.

SERVES 4 to 6

1 small firm white cabbage
4 carrots, peeled and finely grated
6 eating apples, peeled or washed, grated
250g/8oz seedless grapes, cut into halves
90g/3oz raisins
90g/3oz cashew nuts
300ml/10fl oz mayonnaise (page 239)
sea salt and freshly ground black pepper

Cut the cabbage into quarters and remove and discard the hard central core. Thinly slice the leaves into a large mixing bowl. Add the carrot, apple, grapes, raisins and cashew nuts, and bind together with the mayonnaise. Season well and mix again to blend all the ingredients thoroughly. Pile into a large salad bowl, sprinkle on a little more salt, and turn the pepper mill over it a few more times.

CUCUMBER, YOGHURT AND DILL SALAD

This is a really useful dish to have in the refrigerator to accompany or garnish cold meats, fish and pâtés.

SERVES 4

1 cucumber, peeled and finely diced
2 teaspoons sea salt
small bunch fresh dill, washed and chopped
150ml/5fl oz natural yoghurt
1 tablespoon caster sugar
90ml/3fl oz tarragon vinegar
freshly ground black pepper

Put the cucumber into a colander and sprinkle the salt over it. Cover with a plate, weight down with something heavy, and allow to stand for 30 minutes or until the juices have ceased to run.

Put the dill, yoghurt, sugar, vinegar and pepper into a mixing bowl and mix well. Fold in the prepared cucumber and chill in the refrigerator until required.

CARBONNADE OF VEGETABLES WITH CHEESE SCONE TOPPING

When the wind is in a certain direction, it makes our solid-fuel Rayburn cooker roar and sends the temperature gauge right up. Even if this happens at eleven o'clock at night, we cannot let the heat go to waste, so Angela sets to and makes something to go into the oven. Often it is cheese scones, as in this recipe. They freeze well until required, or you can have them for tea next day. Many people cannot believe this is a vegetarian dish, with its rich and malty flavour from the juices of the sautéed vegetables and the yeast extract. Topped with delicious cheese scones it is a substantial and economical dish for almost any occasion.

SERVES 6

FOR THE CARBONNADE:
4 artichoke hearts, peeled and chopped
1 red pepper, deseeded and cut into small pieces
4 carrots, peeled and sliced
2 parsnips, peeled and sliced
2 onions, peeled and chopped
1 leek, finely chopped
2 cloves garlic, crushed with a little salt
4 tablespoons vegetable oil
150ml/5fl oz dry white wine
150ml/5fl oz water
1 tablespoon yeast extract
sea salt and freshly ground black pepper

FOR THE SCONE TOPPING:
125g/4oz wholemeal flour
125g/4oz plain flour
pinch of salt
2 teaspoons baking powder
60g/2oz margarine
90g/3oz Cheddar cheese, grated
150ml/5fl oz milk

First make the carbonnade: put the vegetables into a large saucepan with the garlic. Pour in the oil and sauté for 2 minutes. Stir in the wine, water and yeast extract. Season well, bring to the boil, and simmer for 20 minutes until the vegetables are almost cooked and the sauce thickened. Check the seasonings and pour the mixture into a casserole or earthenware dish and keep warm.

Preheat the oven to 200°C/400°F/gas 6.

Then make the scones: sift the flours, salt and baking powder together into a mixing bowl. Rub in the margarine and cheese, reserving 3 tablespoons of cheese for sprinkling over the top of the scones. Mix in sufficient milk to make a smooth, firm dough, reserving 2 or 3 tablespoons for glazing. Roll out the dough about 1cm/½ inch thick. Cut out 5cm/2-inch circles, using a wine glass or pastry cutter. Lay the scones around the edge of the casserole, keeping the centre clear. Brush the scones with the reserved milk and sprinkle the reserved grated cheese over the top of them. Place the casserole in the preheated oven for 15 minutes to heat the vegetables and bake the scones.

GOUGÈRE OF CHESTNUTS
AND MUSHROOMS

Gougère is a cheese-flavoured choux pastry, and it is very versatile. You can have great fun experimenting with fillings, as we do when the seasons change, or when summer vegetables such as tomatoes, courgettes, marrow and broad beans are abundant. This filling, however, is for when vegetables are rather sparse at the end of winter and just before spring. You need an ovenproof glass pie dish for this recipe because it conducts the heat better than an ordinary ceramic ovenproof dish.

SERVES 4

FOR THE GOUGÈRE:
60g/2oz butter
150ml/5fl oz water
75g/2½oz plain flour
2 free-range eggs, beaten
90g/3oz Gruyère cheese, grated

FOR THE FILLING:
4 tablespoons vegetable oil
1 medium onion, peeled and finely chopped
250g/8oz button mushrooms, sliced
1 clove garlic, crushed with a little salt
1 tin (250g/8oz) whole chestnuts or 10 whole fresh chestnuts,
boiled and peeled
1 tablespoon plain flour
150ml/5fl oz vegetable stock
90g/3oz pecan nuts, broken into pieces, toasted
sea salt and freshly ground black pepper
1 tablespoon chopped fresh parsley to garnish

First make the gougère: put the butter and water into a saucepan and bring to the boil. Remove from the heat and add the flour, beating until the mixture is smooth and does not stick to the sides of the pan. Allow to cool a little, then add the beaten eggs, a little at a time. Beat in 60g/2oz of the Gruyère cheese, reserving the remainder for topping. Grease a 1.25-litre/2-pint pie dish and spoon the gougère mixture around the edge, leaving a gap in the centre for the filling.

Preheat the oven to 200°C/400°F/gas 6.

To make the filling: put the oil into a saucepan, add the onion and cook until soft. Add the mushrooms, garlic and chestnuts, and mix well together. Stir in the flour. The mixture may look a little dry at this stage, but do not worry. Cook for a couple of minutes. Pour in the stock, bring to the boil and cook until the liquid has thickened. Add the pecan nuts and seasonings, and pour the filling into the centre of the pie dish. Sprinkle over the reserved cheese. Bake in the preheated oven for 45 minutes until the gougère is well risen, crusty and golden. Remove from the oven, sprinkle with the parsley and serve at once.

TOMATO CRUMBLE PIE

A well-flavoured tomato is essential for this dish. The usual insipid tomatoes we now find in supermarkets have no smell and little or no flavour. Surprising, really, since they are often labelled 'grown for flavour'. Are tomatoes without this label grown for tasteless-ness? And what is a 'gourmet' tomato? And how about 'living lettuce'? I asked our local supermarket product manager what he considered a 'dead' lettuce to be but there was no answer. While we are trying our best to get supermarkets to stock real, summer-scented, greenhouse-grown tomatoes, it is best (if you have the time) to buy from local growers, or from anyone who puts their own home-grown vegetables on a table outside their garden gate. If you see home produce like this, it is well worth stopping the car for a look through the brown bags filled with surprises: cucumbers, lettuces, half a dozen brown, fresh, free-range eggs at 50p, and even, we hope, a bag of warm, sweet-scented, deep red tomatoes that evoke long-past memories of summer salads for tea on a Sunday afternoon.

SERVES 3 to 4

180ml/6fl oz vegetable oil
175g/6oz breadcrumbs
750g/1½ lb tomatoes, skinned (page 12), deseeded and roughly chopped
1 clove garlic, crushed with a little salt
1 tablespoon chopped fresh basil or tarragon
1 level tablespoon tomato purée
1 teaspoon sugar
sea salt and freshly ground black pepper
90g/3oz Gruyère cheese, grated

Put the oil into a frying pan and fry the breadcrumbs until golden-brown and crunchy. Remove from the pan.

Preheat the oven to 180°C/350°F/gas 4.

Butter a deep 1.1-litre/2-pint pie dish and layer the bottom with half the fried breadcrumbs. Put the tomatoes into a bowl with the garlic, herb, tomato purée, sugar, and salt and pepper to taste. Blend well together. Put this tomato mixture into the breadcrumbed pie dish and sprinkle the remaining half of the breadcrumbs over the top. Scatter the grated cheese evenly over the breadcrumbs, and bake in the preheated oven for 25 minutes until the cheese has melted and is a bubbling golden-brown. Serve as a vegetarian main dish or as a vegetable accompaniment.

MUSHROOM AND POTATO CASSEROLE

This versatile casserole can be served as an accompaniment to a main dish or as a main dish in itself. As a main course, serve a tossed green salad to go with it.

**SERVES 6 AS AN ACCOMPANIMENT,
4 AS A MAIN COURSE**

500g/1lb new potatoes
60g/2oz unsalted butter
250g/8oz baby onions, skins removed
2 sticks celery, finely chopped
1 small clove garlic, crushed with a little salt
250g/8oz button mushrooms, wiped clean if necessary
450ml/15fl oz milk
1 tablespoon potato flour, mixed to a smooth paste with
a little water
freshly grated nutmeg
sea salt and freshly ground black pepper
2 sprigs fresh rosemary
150ml/5fl oz double cream

Wash the potatoes if necessary and steam with the skins on until almost cooked. Allow to cool a little, then remove and discard the skins. Set the potatoes aside.

Preheat the oven to 180°C/350°F/gas 4.

Melt the butter in a saucepan and add the whole baby onions. Lightly brown them. Add the celery, garlic and mushrooms, stir well and cook for a couple of minutes. Pour in the milk and the potato flour paste and cook until the mixture is just beginning to thicken, then add nutmeg and seasonings to taste. Pour into a casserole dish. Put in the skinned potatoes, push in the sprigs of

Fillet of Trout with Fresh Dill and Spinach Sauce (page 66)

Leek and Lovage Soup (page 5)

Chilled Ham Mousse (page 26)

Venison and Beef Steak Suet Crust Pudding (page 126)

Salmon Quenelles with Orange Sauce (page 62)

Harvest Roulade (page 192)

Lime and Lemon Curd Tartlets (page 198)

Chicken in Fresh Peach Sauce (page 86)

rosemary and bake in the preheated oven for 35 to 40 minutes. Test by pushing a knife into an onion: if it goes through easily the casserole is ready. Remove from the oven, discard the rosemary and stir in the cream. Check the seasonings and serve.

LITTLE GEM VEGETABLE PIES

For a time we ran a children's cookery school, held every Saturday, which was very popular. The children were aged four years upwards. They would make these little pies and, with any spare pastry, create a decoration of their own choice to sit on top. We had pastry mice, hens and a tiny fat snowman (which its maker insisted was a robin). The pies were a great success and the children loved learning about the different ingredients and where they came from. We have slightly altered the recipe from the original by adding asparagus to the vegetables. A sorrel or a spinach sauce (page 246) would go well with the pies.

SERVES 4

30g/1oz unsalted butter
4 shallots, peeled and chopped
4 asparagus spears, stems chopped, tips reserved
1 lettuce heart (Little Gem), finely chopped
250g/8oz cooked potato, diced
90g/3oz blue cheese, crumbled
1 free-range egg, beaten
sea salt and freshly ground black pepper
2 × recipe quantity of Cheddar cheese pastry (page 235)
beaten egg to glaze

Preheat the oven to 200°C/400°F/gas 6.

Melt the butter in a saucepan and add the shallots and asparagus stems. Cook until just beginning to soften, then remove from the heat. Put the lettuce, potato and cheese into a bowl. Add the shallot and asparagus and mix together. Add the beaten egg, season to taste and stir to bind the mixture well.

Roll out the pastry until large enough to cut out 8 circles about 12cm/5 inches in diameter. Divide the filling equally between 4 of the pastry circles. Wet the edge of the pastry, then place the remaining circles on top to make 4 pies. Nip the edges together and cut a cross shape into the top. Brush the pies with beaten egg and place on a baking tray. Bake in the preheated oven for 20 minutes or until the pastry is a light golden-brown. Do not overcook or the pastry will develop a bitter taste.

Remove the pies from the oven and keep warm. Steam the asparagus tips for a few minutes, then place a tip on top of each pie and serve.

SPINACH AND HAZELNUT ROULADE

During an Easter snowstorm in our early days at Rockley, when we ran our restaurant in a former chapel, we found a featherless baby rook, blown down along with its nest from the nearby beech trees. As no parents were around and it was blowing and snowing hard, we had no choice but to pick up the tiny pink bundle and keep it warm and fed at home. And so we came to be her family for the next three and a half years. After a shaky beginning Rookley, as we named her, grew rapidly, and we built her a shelter at the bottom of the garden next to the vegetable plot. On fine days, Rookley would hop about picking up earthworms from the garden while we pulled up carrots, potatoes or spinach, which grew well in the fertile soil. Rookley followed Angela wherever she went. She decided one day that rather than fly after Angela as she cycled to the chapel with her vegetables, she would take a ride on the handlebars. This developed into a habit, and so she travelled with us to the restaurant every day, squawking loudly as she rode in style down Rockley Lane, much to the surprise of passing ramblers.

SERVES 4

250g/8oz spinach, steamed
30g/1oz butter
½ teaspoon freshly grated nutmeg
5 free-range eggs, separated
sea salt and freshly ground black pepper
60g/2oz chopped hazelnuts

FOR THE FILLING:
90ml/3fl oz vegetable oil
1 small onion, peeled and finely chopped
4 tablespoons cornflour

150ml / 10fl oz milk
60g / 2oz chopped hazelnuts, toasted
sea salt and freshly ground black pepper
4 tablespoons double cream

Line a Swiss roll tin with a layer of lightly greased baking parchment, allowing the edges to come up above the sides of the tin. Set aside. Wash the spinach, remove any thick stalks and steam the leaves until soft but still bright green. Remove from the pan, put into a colander and squeeze out excess moisture. Put the strained spinach into a liquidizer or food processor with the butter and nutmeg. Blend until the mixture is smooth and creamy. Pour the egg yolks into the spinach mixture, season to taste and blend again. Transfer the mixture to a large bowl, stir in the hazelnuts and set aside while making the filling.

Preheat the oven to 180°C/350°F/gas 4.

To make the filling: put the oil into a saucepan, add the onion and cook until soft. Mix the cornflour with the milk, then add to the pan. Cook until it begins to thicken. Add the toasted hazelnuts, season to taste, then spoon in the cream. Cook for a further few minutes until the sauce is fairly thick but spreadable. Set aside while completing the roulade.

Whisk the egg whites until stiff but not dry, then fold them a little at a time into the spinach mixture. Pour the mixture into the prepared Swiss roll tin. Shake the mixture level in the tin; do not spread with a knife because this removes many of the air bubbles. Bake for 15 to 20 minutes until set. The roulade should feel dry to the touch when ready, particularly in the centre.

Put a piece of greaseproof paper on top of a tea towel. Turn the cooked roulade out on to the paper and remove the original piece of lining paper. Spread the filling on to the roulade. (You may not need all the filling, so serve what is left as a sauce by adding a little milk, seasoning again to taste and reheating.) Roll up the roulade from the long side, removing the paper from underneath as you go. Serve whole on a warmed serving dish.

BAKED ASPARAGUS AND CARROT TIMBALES

One of the attractions of this dish is the beautiful colour of the two vegetable purées. You can experiment with your own choices of compatible vegetable, such as pea with carrot, broccoli with cauliflower, Brussels sprout with potato. If you use spinach or cabbage, drain the cooked leaves very well so that they are not at all wet. The other joy of these timbales is that they can be used as a main course for vegetarians, as a vegetable accompaniment to a main meal, or as a delicious first course. Served with a salad and a sauce, such as spinach sauce (page 246) or green pea and spring onion sauce (page 244), they make an eye-catching dish, and a wholesome one into the bargain.

SERVES 4 AS A STARTER, 2 AS A MAIN COURSE

butter for greasing
2 small free-range eggs
120ml / 4fl oz double cream
125g / 4oz carrots, peeled, cooked and puréed
125g / 4oz thin asparagus, cooked, tops reserved for garnish, stems puréed
sea salt and freshly ground black pepper
pinch of ground cumin
little freshly grated nutmeg
sprigs fresh herbs to garnish

Preheat the oven to 180°C/350°F/gas 4. Line the bases of 4 × 150ml/5fl oz timbale moulds with circles of greaseproof paper lightly greased with butter.

Beat 1 egg and add it, together with half the cream, to the carrot purée. Add the other egg and the remaining cream to the asparagus purée. Add the seasonings and spices to both purées, then liquidize each separately.

Cut the asparagus tips in half lengthways and arrange them around the sides of each timbale mould, distributing them evenly. Pour alternate layers of the purées into each mould, starting with the thicker of the two on the bottom. Pour boiling water into a roasting pan and place the timbales carefully in the pan. The water should come about halfway up the moulds. Cook in the preheated oven for about 35 minutes or until set.

Gently run a knife around the side of each mould to loosen the timbales, then turn out on to a serving dish. Remove the greaseproof paper and garnish with any small sprig of fresh herb you may have in the kitchen. Serve with the salad or sauce accompaniment of your choice.

RED PEPPER AND LEEK SOUFFLÉS

These soufflés are for when friends visit and you eat informally in the kitchen, because they must be served and eaten immediately. Before baking, sprinkle the grated cheese in the centre of each soufflé, not around the edge where it will prevent it from rising. Make certain, too, that the soufflés will not touch the upper shelf in the oven when risen. This stops them from rising properly and makes it difficult to remove them from the oven. Accompany the soufflés with a three-pepper salad (yellow, red, and green), tossed in a good olive oil dressing.

MAKES 4

30g/1oz melted butter, to grease the ramekins
90ml/3fl oz oil
1 medium leek (about 125g/4oz), finely chopped
½ small red pepper, deseeded and very thinly sliced
30g/1oz butter
90ml/3fl oz milk
2 free-range eggs, separated
175g/6oz Cheddar cheese, grated
sea salt and freshly ground black pepper
pinch of cayenne pepper

Preheat the oven to 200°C/400°F/gas 6. Grease 4 individual ramekins, 5cm/4 inches deep, with the melted butter and set aside.

Put the oil into a frying pan and fry the leek and red pepper until soft. Drain and set aside to cool. Melt the butter in a saucepan over a low heat and pour in the milk. Beat in the egg yolks and 150g/5oz of the grated cheese. Season with salt, pepper and cayenne pepper. Stir the mixture until it reaches a smooth, creamy consistency, without allowing it to boil. Then add the red pepper and leek, remove from the heat and allow to cool.

Once the soufflé mixture has cooled, whisk the egg whites until you have a firm snow: you should be able to turn the bowl over without the mixture dropping out. If in doubt, beat on. Cut and fold the beaten egg whites into the soufflé mixture. When well blended, fill the greased ramekins about two-thirds full with the mixture. Sprinkle the remaining Cheddar cheese over the centre and bake in the middle of the preheated oven for 15 to 20 minutes until well risen and a pale golden-brown. Serve at once.

SMOKED GOAT'S CHEESE SOUFFLÉS

We buy all the smoked products for our restaurant from Minola, the farmhouse smokery at Lechlade in Gloucestershire. They use genuine old-fashioned smoking methods with smoke pots and whole English oak logs. This gives their produce, and ultimately our own recipes, a unique flavour. This goat's cheese soufflé is very good served as a first course (1 each) or as a main course (2 each) with a green leaves and hazelnut salad tossed in hazelnut oil dressing. The great joy of this recipe is that it can be made and cooked in advance and then put into the oven to reheat and rise when required; sheer bliss for anyone who entertains. The soufflés also keep well, covered and refrigerated, for 2 to 3 days after the first cooking.

MAKES 8

30g/1oz melted butter, to grease the ramekins
45g/1½oz butter
45g/1½oz plain flour
300ml/10fl oz milk
125g/4oz smoked goat's cheese
1 teaspoon English mustard
3 large free-range eggs, separated
¼ teaspoon ground mace
sea salt and freshly ground black pepper
240ml/8fl oz single cream

Grease 8 ramekins, 3.5cm/1½ inches deep, with the melted butter and set aside.

Melt the 45g/1½oz butter in a saucepan, add the flour and cook until the mixture lightens in colour. Remove from the heat. Pour the milk gradually into the flour and butter mixture, beating well after each addition. Continue beating until all the milk has been used and is completely blended into the mixture. Return to the heat and cook until the mixture begins to bubble, then remove from the heat and add the goat's cheese, mustard, egg yolks, ground mace and salt and pepper to taste. Mix well together (in a food processor if you have one).

Preheat the oven to 180°C/350°F/gas 5.

Whisk the egg whites until you have a firm snow: you should be able to turn the bowl over without the mixture dropping out. If in doubt, beat on. Cut and fold the beaten egg white into the soufflé mixture. When well blended, fill the greased ramekins about two-thirds full with the mixture.

Pour boiling water into a roasting pan and place the ramekins carefully in the tin. The water should come about halfway up the ramekins. Bake for 15 minutes: the soufflés should be soft and lightly browned.

Remove the ramekins from the tin and allow the soufflés to relax. When almost cold, run a knife around the edge of each soufflé to loosen it from the side of the ramekin and tip it out carefully into the palm of your hand. Place the soufflés on a tray. At this stage you can cover the soufflés and keep them in the refrigerator until required.

When required, preheat the oven to 220°C/425°F/gas 7. Remove the soufflés from the refrigerator and place them in a shallow heatproof dish. Spoon a little single cream over them, grind over a few turns of the pepper mill and bake in the preheated oven for 10 minutes or until puffed up and golden-brown. Take care not to overcook or the soufflés will become rubbery. Serve at once.

BEEF TOMATOES FILLED WITH MINTED PEA PURÉE

If fresh peas are not in season, use frozen (but never tinned) for this recipe. Fresh Parmesan cheese is another important ingredient: please do not use pre-grated cheese in tubs, which tastes just like its packaging. Chopped celery is optional but gives a nice crunch to the purée. When fresh peas are in season, serve the filled tomatoes surrounded by a moat of puréed fresh peas and a few thinly sliced spring onions with a little hazelnut oil drizzled over.

SERVES 4 AS A STARTER, 2 AS A MAIN COURSE

4 ripe, firm beef tomatoes
90ml/3fl oz olive oil
1 small clove garlic, crushed with a little salt
freshly ground black pepper
500g/1lb shelled peas or fresh petits pois
30g/1oz butter
10 leaves fresh mint, plus a few extra for garnishing
120ml/4fl oz single cream
1 stick celery, finely chopped (optional)
60g/2oz fresh Parmesan cheese, grated
90g/3oz cashew nuts, chopped

Preheat the oven to 180°C/350°F/gas 4.

Stand the tomatoes on their flattest end and cut off a slice from the top. Scoop out and discard the central core and seeds. Tip out any juice remaining inside the tomatoes. Brush the insides with the oil and smear a little crushed garlic inside each one, then grind pepper over them.

Steam the peas until tender, then liquidize with the butter, mint and cream until you have a smooth purée. Add the celery, if using, and fill the tomatoes with the mixture.

Mix together the Parmesan cheese and cashew nuts, and pile a little on top of each tomato: it should cling to the pea purée. Place on a baking tray and bake in the preheated oven for 20 to 25 minutes until the cheese has melted and is a light golden-brown. Garnish with the extra mint leaves and serve at once.

SAVOURY BAKED COURGETTES

'Why is everyone sitting in their car?' came a voice from the kitchen. Six or seven cars and their occupants were waiting in the car park. It was a quarter to eight on a Saturday night, and most of our guests had booked for half past seven. 'Maybe they are waiting for their guests to arrive before coming into the restaurant,' I replied. They continued to sit in their cars, however, and so after a while I sallied forth and asked if they thought we had turned into a drive-in restaurant and would they like dinner in their cars? It transpired that although I had unlocked the dining-room door, I had not unbolted the outer porch door. Having tried the door, the first guests decided we were not quite ready, and so sat in their cars, passing this message on to others as they arrived. It must say something about the British character. I sheepishly unbolted the door and the evening began. We then, of course, had everything to do all at once. This dish is excellent for entertaining because the preparation can be done up to the baking stage and the dish put into the oven as soon your guests arrive – providing they can get in.

SERVES 4

4 good-sized courgettes
150ml/5fl oz olive oil
freshly ground black pepper
1 onion, peeled and finely chopped
8 button mushrooms, finely chopped
1 clove garlic, crushed with a little salt
1 tablespoon fresh thyme leaves
6 fresh dates, stoned and chopped

Wash the courgettes and cut a slice along the length of each one to form a lid. Scoop out the flesh with a teaspoon, taking care not to break through the sides, and place the flesh into a bowl. Rub 1 to 2 tablespoons of the oil inside and all over the outside of each courgette. Season each cavity with pepper and place in an ovenproof dish.

Preheat the oven to 180°C/350°F/gas 4.

Put the remaining oil into a saucepan, add the onion, and cook until soft. Put in the courgette flesh, mushrooms, garlic and thyme. Cook slowly, stirring from time to time, until the mushrooms release their juices. Add the dates, blend all the ingredients well together and remove from the heat. Divide the mixture evenly between the courgettes, pouring any juices around them. Put the courgette lids on, cover the dish with kitchen foil and bake in the preheated oven for 35 to 40 minutes. Serve at once.

QUAIL EGGS DUBARRY

On one of our regular visits to Chilton kitchen gardens to collect our vegetables, we were met by Harry Dodson, the head gardener, and his wife, Jane. Harry approached with two young, succulent, creamy-white cauliflowers. They looked like two white clouds caught in a nest of leaves. 'They are not very big,' Harry apologized. We brought them home, steamed them and ate them *au naturel*, and they were the most delicious cauliflowers we had tasted for years. Buy cauliflowers that look bright and vigorous and have a good fresh smell. If the poor thing looks tired and dejected, with brown curling leaves and a dank aroma, it is best left on the shelf. If you wish, serve this dish piled into a cheese tartlet case (page 235).

SERVES 4

12 fresh quail eggs
300ml/10fl oz béchamel sauce (page 240)
1 small firm cauliflower
3 courgettes, washed and grated
small knob of butter
sea salt and freshly ground black pepper
1 tablespoon chopped fresh coriander or parsley

Put the quail eggs into simmering water and boil until hard: about 2 minutes. Do not overboil or the yolks will turn black. Plunge the eggs at once into cold water to prevent further cooking. Remove the shells.

Make the béchamel sauce and keep warm in a double saucepan, or in a pan set over a larger pan of simmering water.

Break the cauliflower florets from the stalk. Slice the stalk thinly into strips and set aside. Steam the cauliflower florets, then roughly chop them and add to the béchamel sauce.

Steam the grated courgette and cauliflower stalks together. Turn out into a bowl, toss with the butter and season to taste. Pile a nest of courgette and cauliflower stalk on to each dinner plate and place 3 quail eggs on top. Stir the sauce, then pour it over the eggs. Sprinkle with the coriander or parsley and serve.

CELERIAC AND CASHEW NUT PATTIES

These delicious little patties were initially intended as a vegetable accompaniment to our restaurant meat dishes, but they have since become a main dish in their own right. One evening when the restaurant was very busy, the vegetarian dish that Angela had prepared had all gone and a young girl decided there and then that she was vegetarian and would on no account eat fish or meat. So Angela quickly made a simple watercress sauce and served the vegetable patties as a main dish. They were greatly enjoyed, and so a vegetarian dish was born which now regularly appears on the menu. The patties are very easy to make. Serve with a sauce of your choice, such as sorrel or spinach (page 246).

SERVES 4

120ml/4fl oz vegetable oil
1 medium clove garlic, crushed with a little salt
1 large onion, peeled and sliced
1 celeriac, peeled and thinly sliced
60g/2oz cashew nuts, chopped and lightly toasted
about 40 leaves fresh lovage, finely chopped
good pinch of mace
125g/4oz wholemeal breadcrumbs
1 small free-range egg, beaten
sea salt and freshly ground black pepper
a little vegetable oil to fry the patties

Pour the oil into a large saucepan and add the garlic, onion and celeriac. Stir, cover with a lid, and cook over a medium heat just long enough to soften the vegetables. When checking the vegetables to see if they are ready, lift the lid and allow the condensation to drip into the pan: this prevents the vegetables from sticking to the bottom.

Remove the pan from the heat and allow the vegetables to cool a little, then liquidize them to a rough purée (you need a little texture in the patties). Turn the purée into a bowl and stir in the cashew nuts, lovage, mace and breadcrumbs. Blend well together. Add the beaten egg and mix it in well with the seasonings. Allow the mixture to cool, then with floured hands form into patties about 2.5cm/1 inch thick. Wrap in clingfilm and leave in the refrigerator to chill.

When required, fry the patties in a little vegetable oil on both sides until light brown.

PARSNIP AND CELERIAC PATTIES

Parsnips have had an undeservedly poor reputation, so much so that by the sixteenth century they were thought fit only for animal feed. Fortunately the humble parsnip is now held in higher esteem. In an American recipe we have they are cooked with brown sugar and orange juice to develop a lovely glaze. These patties make an excellent vegetarian entrée or main course, and are suitable for lunch or dinner. They are also good made bite-size and served as canapés. And they are perfect to convert anyone who remembers school dinners with parsnips tasting like stewed wool and believes they don't like the vegetable at all. Unless very bruised or marked, parsnips need not be peeled, just scrubbed clean and topped and tailed. Unless they are huge, they do not need to be cut up and their woody core removed. If you serve parsnips as a side dish, remember the advice of the late Jane Grigson: 'never serve them straight from the water, any more than you would appear at the dinner table dripping from a bath. Only asparagus and Aphrodite can get away with it' (*Jane Grigson's Vegetable Book*, 1978).

SERVES 4

30g / 1oz unsalted butter
30g / 1oz plain flour
150ml / 5fl oz milk
sea salt and freshly ground black pepper
250g / 8oz parsnips, cooked and puréed
250g / 8oz celeriac, cooked and puréed
60g / 2oz pecan nuts, chopped
1 free-range egg, beaten
wholemeal breadcrumbs for coating
oil for deep-frying (see pages xii–xiii)

Melt the butter in a small saucepan and stir in the flour. Pour in the milk and bring to the boil, stirring all the time. Season well.

Put the cooked and puréed parsnips and celeriac into the sauce. Sprinkle in the pecan nuts and mix well together. Turn the mixture out on to a board and spread out to form a flat cake. Allow to cool. When cold, form into small patties of the required size. Place the beaten egg and the breadcrumbs in separate shallow dishes. Dip the patties in the beaten egg, roll in the breadcrumbs and deep-fry in hot oil until golden-brown. Serve at once.

POTATO, MINT AND
GHERKIN LOAF

Easter: a time of new growth, green shoots, weddings, and *al fresco* meals in the garden. Last year we catered for an early spring wedding when the sun shone warmly and the guests were able to take their champagne out on to the lawn and toast the bride and groom under the freshly sprouting oak tree. Among the chilled mousses, salmon and soufflés of our cold buffet was this versatile potato loaf. You can add chopped ham or chicken, but we kept it vegetarian for this event. (If you are not making a vegetarian loaf, you can use gelatine instead of arrowroot.) This loaf can be made a day in advance. For a buffet table, set it upon a bed of fresh green lettuce leaves and garnish with sprigs of mint and chive flowers.

SERVES 6 to 8

500g/1lb potatoes, peeled and cut into small cubes
300ml/10fl oz milk
2 teaspoons arrowroot, mixed to a paste with 120ml/4fl oz water
4 spring onions, chopped
3 pickled gherkins, chopped
2 tablespoons chopped fresh mint
3 tablespoons mayonnaise
3 tablespoons fromage frais
sea salt and freshly ground black pepper
cayenne pepper
lettuce, mint and chive flowers to garnish

Put the potato cubes into a saucepan, pour on the milk and cook slowly until the potatoes are almost tender. Pour in the arrowroot paste, stirring well, and continue to cook briefly until the potatoes are cooked and the mixture has thickened. Transfer the potatoes to a mixing bowl, add the spring onion, gherkin and mint and mix well together. Allow to cool a little, then fold in the mayonnaise and fromage frais. Blend thoroughly. Season to taste with salt, pepper and cayenne pepper, and stir again.

Line a 500g/1lb loaf tin with greaseproof paper and spoon the loaf mixture into it. Allow to set in the refrigerator (2 to 3 hours, or overnight if you prefer). Turn out on to a bed of fresh green leaves, remove the greaseproof paper and garnish the loaf with mint and chive flowers. When ready to serve, cut into slices.

POTATO AND STILTON CROQUETTES

This recipe came about by chance when we had last-minute bookings for dinner. The restaurant became busier and busier as the evening went by, and the vegetarian dish ran out. Angela was called upon to improvise. Creamed potatoes were already prepared as a vegetable, so a few spoonfuls were borrowed and formed into a ball. Stilton was also to hand, so a piece of cheese was put into the centre of the potato ball, which was then coated with breadcrumbs and deep-fried. We made a number of these and they were a great success. These croquettes can be made with a variety of fillings, such as cream cheese, smoked goat's cheese or garlic-flavoured mushrooms. We have found that surrounding the filling with a spinach leaf helps to keep it in place and also allows you to see where the potato covering may be too thin. After deep-frying, these potato croquettes can be kept warm in the oven until required. They can also be frozen after being coated in breadcrumbs.

MAKES 12

2kg/4lb floury potatoes, peeled
2 free-range eggs, beaten
30g/1oz butter
½ teaspoon sea salt
½ teaspoon freshly ground white pepper
90g/3oz toasted almonds
175g/6oz Stilton cheese (15g/½oz for each croquet)
12 small fresh spinach leaves, washed
2 small free-range eggs, beaten, for coating
250g/8oz breadcrumbs for coating
oil for deep-frying (see pages xii–xiii)

Boil the potatoes, drain and cream with the beaten eggs, butter, salt and pepper. Blend the toasted almonds in evenly. Form into 12 egg-shaped croquettes.

Wrap each 15g/½oz piece of Stilton in a spinach leaf. Make a small nest in the centre of each potato croquette and push in the filling. Squeeze the potato gently together to enclose the filling.

Place the beaten egg and the breadcrumbs in separate shallow dishes. Roll the croquettes one at a time in the beaten egg until completely covered. With forks or tongs lift out the croquette and toss in the breadcrumbs, gently pressing the crumbs on to the potato. Deep-fry in hot oil until golden-brown. Serve at once, unless the croquettes are to be kept warm in the oven, in which case take care not to over-fry or they will become hard.

PEPPERED CREAMED POTATO CAKES

Good-quality ingredients are essential in all recipes, and the potatoes for this one are no exception.

SERVES 4 to 6

*500g/1lb floury potatoes, peeled, boiled in salted water
and roughly chopped
30g/1oz butter
½ clove garlic, crushed with a little salt
90ml/3fl oz single cream
1 small free-range egg, beaten
sea salt and freshly ground white pepper
2 tablespoons black peppercorns, crushed
60g/2oz fine breadcrumbs
1 small free-range egg, beaten, for coating
a little vegetable oil for frying*

Push the cooked potatoes through a ricer or sieve into a bowl. Add the butter, garlic, cream, 1 egg, salt and white pepper. Mix together well. In a separate bowl, mix the peppercorns with the breadcrumbs. Form the potato into 8 or 12 evenly sized cakes about 1cm/just under ½ inch thick. Allow to cool completely.

Dip the potato cakes one at a time into the beaten egg. Using a pair of forks, remove the cakes and toss them in the peppercorn and breadcrumb mixture, making sure there are no bare patches. Use a pastry brush to paint with a little more egg if there should be any patches. Repeat the process until all the potato cakes are completely coated in the peppered crumbs.

Pour the oil into a frying pan and fry the potato cakes on both sides until golden-brown. Keep warm until required.

DUCHESSE POTATOES

We serve these potatoes quite often in our restaurant because they can be made in the afternoon and then baked to order in the evening. They enhance the look of the main dish, stay hot while the rest of the main course is being served, and are delicious. A well-flavoured potato is important. Do not use a waxy variety, which will not cream easily. When piped into their pyramid shape (you need a piping bag with a star nozzle for this), before baking, they can also be frozen until required.

SERVES 8 (2 DUCHESSE POTATOES EACH)

1kg/2lb floury potatoes, boiled in salted water and drained
60g/2oz butter
2 small free-range eggs, beaten
120ml/4fl oz single cream or milk
sea salt and freshly ground black pepper

Put the cooked potatoes through a ricer or sieve. Add the butter, two-thirds of the beaten eggs, the cream or milk and seasonings, and beat well until the mixture is smooth.

Preheat the oven to 180°C/350°F/gas 4.

Put a spoonful of creamed potato into a piping bag with a star nozzle and pipe on to a greased baking tray in a pyramid rosette about 5cm/2 inches high. Continue until all the potato is used up, making 16 pyramids in all. Brush with the remaining beaten egg and bake in the top of the preheated oven for about 25 minutes until golden-brown.

6

Puddings

APRICOT COURTESIES

Apricots, as the wise man knows,
Is sweeter when the colour glows.
'Be kind and courteous to this gentleman; Hop in his walks, and gambol in his eyes; Feed him with apricocks, and dewberries.' These are the courtesies that Shakespeare puts into the mouth of Titania when she is telling her fairies how to greet the wayfarer in *A Midsummer Night's Dream*. Quick and easy to make, apricot courtesies can be prepared for unexpected guests.

MAKES 6

6 fresh apricots
175g/6oz almond paste
250g/8oz puff pastry
1 free-range egg, beaten
icing sugar to finish (optional)

Preheat the oven to 200°C/400°F/gas 6.

Cut a little way into each apricot to remove the stone.

Divide the almond paste into 6 equal pieces. Push each lump of paste into the centre of a stoned apricot and push the fruit gently together to seal in the paste.

Divide the pastry into 6 small pieces. Roll out a piece on a floured board. Place an apricot in the centre and bring the pastry edges together to cover the fruit completely. With the thumb and forefinger gently press the pastry together to form a short stalk. Repeat with the remaining apricots and pastry. If any pastry is left over, cut out small leaves and gently fix to the stalk.

Brush each parcel with the beaten egg and place on a dampened baking tray. Bake in the preheated oven for 15 to 20 minutes, until the pastry is golden-brown. Remove from the oven, dust with icing sugar if desired, and serve with double or single cream.

CHRISTMAS PUDDING 1994

1994 was our first Christmas in our new restaurant and to celebrate the occasion Angela made a special Christmas pudding. Eating habits have changed over the years, so those heavy puddings that left us feeling quite blown and bloated are largely a thing of the past. This pudding has a rich flavour and a dark colour, but it is light on the digestive system. After our Christmas Day lunch, many of our restaurant guests asked for the recipe, and here it is. It really is well worth all the ingredients, all the mixing and especially all the steaming – it is the steaming time that makes for a rich, moist, dark pudding. The dark ale Old Peculier is most important; there really is no substitute. Other dark ales just do not give this pudding its special flavour. Most supermarkets and wine merchants now stock Old Peculier. If you have trouble finding it, write to Theakston's Brewery at Masham, Yorkshire, and they will tell you the whereabouts of your nearest stockist. You can make the pudding well in advance. Mature it for up to 2 months in the refrigerator, and then freeze it until Christmas comes: most homes these days are too warm to allow the pudding to be stored in a pantry. This recipe makes several puddings – ideal for gifts.

MAKES 3 LARGE PUDDINGS, OR 2 LARGE AND 2 SMALL. ALTERNATIVELY, INDIVIDUAL PUDDINGS CAN BE MADE IN 175 G/6 OZ MOULDS

250g/8oz apricots, chopped
250g/8oz dates, stoned and chopped
250g/8oz prunes, chopped
1.5kg/3lb dried mixed fruit (sultanas, raisins, currants)
60g/2oz crystallized orange peel, finely chopped
250g/8oz Brazil nuts, chopped
750g/1½ lb apples, peeled, cored and grated
250g/8oz carrots, peeled and grated
grated rind and juice of 2 small oranges

grated rind and juice of 2 small lemons
350g/12oz vegetable or beef suet
250g/8oz wholemeal flour
350g/12oz wholemeal breadcrumbs
1 teaspoon baking powder
½ nutmeg, freshly grated
1 teaspoon ground cinnamon
1 teaspoon ground ginger
500g/1lb dark soft brown sugar
5 free-range eggs
120ml/4fl oz dark rum
1 tablespoon black treacle
300ml/10fl oz Old Peculier (dark Yorkshire ale)
4 tablespoons brandy, to serve

Grease your chosen pudding basins with butter. Cut a circle of baking parchment and place at the bottom of each basin to prevent the puddings from sticking when turned out. Set aside.

You need two large and one small mixing bowls for preparing the ingredients. Put the apricots, dates, prunes, mixed fruit, crystallized peel, Brazil nuts, apple, carrot, orange and lemon rind and juice, and the suet into one large bowl. Mix thoroughly together.

Put the flour, breadcrumbs, baking powder, nutmeg, cinnamon, ginger and sugar into the second large bowl. With your hands, mix the ingredients together well, pressing out any large lumps of sugar.

Put the eggs, rum, black treacle and Old Peculier into the small bowl. Beat well until thoroughly blended.

Tip the contents of the second bowl into the first bowl and mix thoroughly until well blended. Add the contents of the third bowl and blend in thoroughly as before.

When all the ingredients are well mixed and there are no dry patches, spoon the mixture into the prepared pudding basins to 2.5cm/1 inch from the top. Cover with a circle of baking parchment and another circle of kitchen foil, making sure it is secure and tight around the rim of the bowl so that water cannot seep into the puddings.

Steam large puddings for 8 hours; small (175g/6oz) puddings for 4 hours. Remove the pudding from the steamer, discard the parchment and foil, run a palette knife around the sides of the pudding to loosen it from the basin, and turn out on to a serving dish. Place a sprig of holly on top.

Warm the brandy in a ladle held over a low heat. When warmed, put a lighted match to the surface of the brandy, and when ignited pour it quickly over the pudding, avoiding the holly. Serve as the brandy burns with a blue flame, turning out any electric lights for maximum effect. If you have a long way to walk with the pudding, use double the amount of brandy to allow it to burn for longer.

COFFEE LIQUEUR AND GINGER CHEESECAKE

'It was a brilliant moonlight night, but extremely cold; our chaise whirled rapidly over the frozen ground; the post-boy smacked his whip incessantly ... "He knows where he is going," said my companion, laughing, "and is eager to arrive in time for some of the merriment and good cheer of the servants' hall."' So Washington Irving describes a homecoming in his book *Old Christmas*. We have had a similar experience, though sadly not in a whirling chaise. When our restaurant was still in the chapel, every year, about a week before Christmas, we would turn it over to the local church and its parishioners for a candle-lit carol service. The last was held on just such a cold and frosty night as that described in *Old Christmas*. The carols had been sung, mulled wine drunk, mince pies eaten, and everyone had made their way home, leaving Angela and me to lock up. That done, we walked down the frosted lane towards our cottage, stopping briefly to look into the deep midwinter sky, its hundreds of stars like points of fire burning through the icy air. At that moment we heard a choir singing. There was no one near, nor any radio or television to intrude on the silence. Just a faint distant singing, which stopped after a few minutes. Had a freak soundwave carried another carol service out into the night air, just as bells can sometimes be heard some distance away? We were not alone in hearing this celestial choir; a friend who lived just along the lane heard it too. We went into our cottage just as friends were arriving to join us for supper, and this was the pudding on that special evening. The usual digestive-biscuit base is replaced by crumbled ginger biscuits, and with the addition of a coffee liqueur such as Tia Maria, or indeed a whisky cream such as Bailey's, it is a marvellous pudding to serve for any special occasion. We always save it for a winter evening around Christmas time, to remind us of the heavenly choir. (See recipe overleaf.)

COFFEE LIQUEUR AND GINGER CHEESECAKE (CONTINUED)

SERVES 6 to 8

butter for greasing the tin
175g/6oz ginger biscuits
60g/2oz butter
300ml/10fl oz milk
90ml/3fl oz strong coffee or coffee essence such as Camp
3 rounded teaspoons powdered gelatine, dissolved in 90ml/3fl oz cold
water
1 miniature bottle (120ml/4fl oz) Tia Maria
90g/3oz light soft brown sugar
500g/1lb full-fat cream cheese
240ml/8fl oz whipping cream

TO DECORATE:
120ml/4fl oz double cream
crystallized ginger pieces
small white or yellow flower

Grease a 20cm/8-inch loose-bottomed cake tin with butter.

Put the ginger biscuits into a strong plastic bag and use a rolling pin to crush them. Melt the butter in a saucepan and stir in the biscuit crumbs. Tip the crumbs into the cake tin and press firmly into the base. Put into the refrigerator to chill.

Boil the milk in a saucepan, remove from the heat, then stir in the coffee. Pour in the dissolved gelatine and the liqueur. Stir well, making sure the gelatine has completely dissolved, then add the sugar and stir again until completely blended.

Put the cream cheese into a food processor or liquidizer, add the coffee and sugar liquid and blend until smooth.

Whip the cream in a fairly large mixing bowl until it just holds its shape. Fold in half the quantity of the coffee and cheese mixture. When blended, fold in the remaining half. Pour into the prepared biscuit base and return to the refrigerator to chill and set (3 to 4 hours).

About 1 hour before serving, remove the cheesecake from the tin, place on a serving dish and bring to room temperature before eating.

Whip the double cream, put into a piping bag with a star nozzle and pipe rosettes around the rim of the cheesecake. Place a piece of crystallized ginger on top of each cream rosette and a few small pieces in the centre of the cake. A small fresh white or yellow flower placed in the centre will complete the presentation.

FRESH PEAR AND GINGER CRUMBLE WITH HIGHLAND MALT CREAM SABAYON

About 6 inches of snow had fallen on top of what had already settled from the previous three days. It was the extremely cold winter of 1981/2. Our small hamlet had been cut off by the snow for three days. No cars or noisy tractors disturbed the sparkling, icy peace. The electricity had been cut off two days back. We were the only people in the village to have a solid-fuel cooker, so each cottage brought their Sunday joint for us to roast in the Rayburn. There were five different cuts of meat, a couple of apple pies and our own pear and ginger crumble. As each joint was cooked, we delivered the meat to its rightful cottage, and were given a glass of good cheer to send us on our way and to say thank you. By the time the final joint was delivered it was 4.30, that bewitching time on a snowy afternoon, when the countryside takes on a blue, icy-cold sparkle. Candles were shining in the cottage windows as we made our way home. The Rayburn had done a good job, and we thanked Providence and the previous tenants of the cottage who had installed the solid-fuel cooker. We settled down to our own candle-lit lunch, still warm in the cooker, at five o'clock. This pudding, as you now know, can be prepared in advance and kept warm in the oven until required. The sabayon sauce that accompanies it is good and warming. Laced with whisky it makes an ideal accompaniment to a variety of puddings, especially on a cold, snowy winter's afternoon.

SERVES 4

FOR THE CRUMBLE:
175g/6oz wholemeal flour
60g/2oz plain flour
¼ teaspoon salt
125g/4oz butter
3 tablespoons demerara sugar

FOR THE FILLING:
1kg/2lb fresh pears, peeled, cored and cut into large pieces
4 whole pieces preserved ginger, sliced
2 tablespoons dark soft brown sugar
grated rind and juice of 1 lemon
1 recipe quantity whisky sabayon sauce (page 254)

Preheat the oven to 180°C/350°F/gas 4.

First make the crumble: sift both flours with the salt into a mixing bowl. Rub the butter lightly into the flour using your fingertips. Continue to mix until the mixture resembles fine breadcrumbs. Add the sugar and mix well in.

Then make the filling: lay the pieces of pear in a pie dish, cover with the slices of preserved ginger and sprinkle over the sugar and the lemon juice and rind.

Spread the crumble mixture evenly over the pears and ginger. Press down lightly: the pudding should have a light, loose topping. Bake the crumble in the preheated oven for 45 minutes or until a lovely golden-brown. Serve hot with the whisky sabayon.

JANUARY PEAR BRANDY FLAN

It was a freezing cold, early January night. Outside hedges, trees, fields and roads were white with frost. We had decided to have a small dinner party for a couple of dear friends who had supported our various restaurants throughout the years. As usual with our impromptu parties, the numbers increased as other loyal friends and customers were invited. The dinner party grew from four to twelve. Four of our guests were coming quite a distance, from Reading and Bath, and the food needed to be such that it would not spoil if they were delayed by icy roads. Buck's Fizz was served on arrival (orange juice only for the drivers of the party), Angela roasted a huge free-range chicken stuffed with fresh rosemary, bacon, chestnuts, onion and sausagemeat, and the pudding was this delicious, quick-to-make pear flan. The pears were poached in a little champagne left over from New Year's Eve. The night was bitterly cold, the food hot, the company warm and friendly, and we remember the evening each time we cook 'January flan'.

MAKES 1 × 35 CM/14 INCH FLAN OR 2 × 18 CM/7 INCH FLANS

500g/1lb shortcrust pastry
150ml/5 fl oz champagne or sparkling wine
juice of 1 lemon
90g/3oz caster sugar
9 or 10 fresh, ripe pears, peeled, cored and cut in half lengthways
2 rounded teaspoons arrowroot, mixed to a paste with a little water
4 tablespoons pear brandy
double cream and a little pear brandy (or Kirsch) to serve

Preheat the oven to 190°C/375°F/gas 5.

Roll out the pastry fairly thinly and use to line the flan dish(es). Line with foil and fill with baking beans, then bake blind in the preheated oven until just golden-brown.

Pour the champagne or sparkling wine, lemon juice and sugar into a saucepan. Stir over a low heat until the sugar has dissolved, then poach the pears gently until heated through but not too soft. Remove the pears, then boil up the syrup until reduced by about one third. Pour in the arrowroot paste and the pear brandy and return to the heat until the syrup begins to thicken.

Lay the pear halves evenly on top of the pastry. Take a sharp knife, slice the pears lengthways, and press gently to fan out the slices slightly. The pear slices should cover the whole of the pastry in the flan dish. Spoon over the poaching liquid and allow to cool. Serve cold, or warm from the oven. Add a little pear brandy or Kirsch to the double cream and serve it separately.

BRANDY-CREAM GINGER SOUFFLÉ

'To choose Eggs at Market: Put the large end of the egg to your tongue; if it feels warm it is new.' This advice, from *A New System of Domestic Cookery*, 1860, is not easily followed today, but clearly worked for our Victorian ancestors. Fortunately, supermarkets and egg farms now date their produce. This soufflé regularly appears on our restaurant menu and always looks wonderfully appetizing. Decorate the top with gold- or silver-coloured sugared almonds and a fresh flower for a special occasion.

SERVES 4

450ml/15fl oz milk
3 free-range eggs, separated
60g/2oz caster sugar
4 tablespoons preserved ginger syrup
15g/½oz gelatine, dissolved in 120ml/4fl oz cold water
150ml/5fl oz double cream
2 tablespoons preserved ginger, thinly sliced

TO DECORATE:
4–6 tablespoons brandy for mixing with the remaining double cream
small slices of preserved ginger
toasted slivered almonds, or gold- and silver-coloured sugared almonds,
and a fresh flower (optional)

Prepare a 600ml/1 pint soufflé dish as described on page xiv.

Put the milk into a saucepan and scald it by heating to just below boiling point. Beat the egg yolks and sugar together until light in colour and thick. Pour in the ginger syrup and hot milk. Return to the pan and stir over a low heat until the mixture begins to thicken (do not boil). Pour the mixture into a bowl and stir in the dissolved gelatine. Cover the custard mixture to prevent a skin from forming.

Whip the cream until it begins to thicken. Whisk the egg whites until stiff but not dry.

Stand the custard in a bowl of cold water containing 3 or 4 ice-cubes and stir until the custard begins to thicken. Using a metal spoon, quickly fold in half the whipped cream, then all the sliced ginger and lastly the whisked egg whites. Stir carefully with the bowl still in the cold water. As the mixture thickens, pour into the prepared soufflé dish and leave in the refrigerator to set.

When the soufflé has set, remove the paper by dipping a palette knife into hot water and slipping the blade between the soufflé and the paper.

To decorate the soufflé: pour the brandy into the remaining cream and whip lightly. Put the whipped cream into a piping bag with a star nozzle and pipe rosettes around the edge of the soufflé. Arrange the slices of ginger, and the almonds, if using, between or on top of the cream rosettes. Rinse a fresh flower, if using, under cold water, shake well and place in the centre of the soufflé.

HOT ORANGE AND DRAMBUIE SOUFFLÉS WITH TANGERINE SABAYON SAUCE

These soufflés – double cooked – are another of those wonderful dishes that can be made in advance. We use double-cooked soufflés, sweet and savoury, a great deal in the restaurant. The first cooking takes the soufflés to their setting stage, when they should be put in the refrigerator until required. The final cooking, for the soufflés to heat through and rise, takes only 10 minutes. Transfer the cooked soufflés to plates (use a fish slice), surround – in this case – with fresh tangerine sabayon sauce, sprinkle with a little icing sugar and serve at once. Use good vanilla – preferably Madagascar Bourbon vanilla extract, which you can buy from Culpeper's herbal shops. Synthetic essence can spoil a dish.

MAKES 7 SMALL SOUFFLÉS

butter for greasing the ramekins
45g/1½oz unsalted butter
45g/1½oz plain flour
200ml/7fl oz milk made up to 300ml/10fl oz with Drambuie
1 teaspoon Madagascar Bourbon vanilla extract
3 large free-range eggs, separated
grated rind of 1 orange
125g/4oz full-fat cream cheese
1 tablespoon caster sugar
1 recipe quantity tangerine sabayon (page 253)

Preheat the oven to 180°C/350°F/gas 4. Grease 7 ramekins, 5cm/2 inches deep, with butter.

Melt the butter in a saucepan over a low heat, taking care not to brown it. Add the flour and stir gently until the mixture takes on a paler colour. Remove from the heat and pour in the flavoured milk, add the vanilla, and stir well until all the liquid has completely blended in. Return to the heat and cook through until the mixture no longer has a floury taste, being careful not to overcook the sauce. When the sauce is smooth, remove from the heat and beat in the egg yolks, orange rind, cream cheese and the caster sugar.

Beat the egg whites until stiff. You should be able to turn the bowl upside down without the egg whites falling out.

Fold the egg white into the soufflé mixture using a fairly large metal spoon. When well blended, pour into the prepared ramekins. Stand the ramekins in a baking pan and pour in boiling water to come only a little way up the dishes. The water prevents the soufflés from drying out. Cook in the preheated oven for 15 to 20 minutes until set and slightly risen. Remove from the oven and allow to cool. The soufflés will shrink slightly at this stage.

When the soufflés are cold, run a knife around the edges to loosen them. Tip them out into the palm of your hand and transfer to a tray. Cover and leave in a cool place until required.

Thirty minutes before serving, preheat the oven to 220°C/425°F/gas 7. Fifteen minutes before serving, sprinkle the soufflés with a little caster or vanilla sugar and place on a greased baking tray. Bake again in the hot oven for about 10 minutes, until risen and golden.

Baked soufflés may sink quite quickly so it is a good idea to cook half the batch a few minutes earlier than the rest, allowing you time to pour the sauce around the first batch while the remaining soufflés are still cooking.

DARK CHOCOLATE PUDDING WITH WHISKY SABAYON SAUCE

The first chocolate house opened in London in 1657, and chocolate soon became a popular hot drink, especially at breakfast-time. It was described as the food of the gods, and was believed to have therapeutic as well as nutritional qualities. During the Victorian era coffee and chocolate houses reached the height of their popularity. They were frequented mostly by men, and were the forerunner of the gentlemen's clubs that provided an escape for men from the cares of the household. This pudding would have been extremely popular with the Victorians, and I believe it is still served from time to time in that great long-established restaurant in the Strand, Simpsons, where some years ago we once had the honour of dining downstairs, not a regular occurrence for women at that time. We had booked lunch at the Savoy but the dining room was closed due to refurbishment. The reception manager booked us into Simpsons, and told them our tale of woe. I think he must have known the head waiter. The whisky sauce turns this traditional nursery pudding into one that would not be out of place at the dinner-party table.

SERVES 4 to 6

butter for greasing the pudding basin
125g/4oz caster sugar
125g/4oz butter
2 free-range eggs, beaten
a few drops of vanilla extract, such as Madagascar Bourbon
60g/2oz dark chocolate
175g/6oz self-raising flour
a little milk to mix
1 recipe quantity whisky sabayon (page 254)

Half-fill a large saucepan or steamer with water and put it on to boil for steaming the pudding. Grease a 750ml/1½ pint pudding basin with butter.

Cream together the sugar and butter until fluffy and pale. Add the eggs and vanilla extract a little at a time, beating well.

Break the chocolate into pieces and place in a small basin. Put the basin over a saucepan filled with hot water. Melt the chocolate over a gentle heat. Pour the melted chocolate into the egg mixture and stir to blend in. Sift the flour and, using a metal spoon, fold half the flour into the egg and chocolate mixture. Add sufficient milk to give a dropping consistency, then fold in the remaining flour and a little extra milk if required to keep a smooth dropping texture.

Pour the mixture into the prepared basin, cover with grease-proof paper and secure with string. Steam for 1½ hours.

When the pudding is ready, serve hot with the whisky sabayon poured over or handed separately in a jug or sauce-boat.

DARK CHOCOLATE AND ORANGE ROULADE

We served this deliciously rich roulade for a dinner party many years ago at an MP's house in Somerset. Before dinner, the hostess took me into a large cupboard lined with shelves, on which were piles of plates of almost every size and shape. Climbing on to a stool, she reached up for a pile of pudding plates, fourteen to be exact. On handing me the precarious pile, she casually said, 'Don't drop them, they are over two hundred years old.' We did not drop them, and the roulade took on a very regal appearance on these antique dishes. This roulade must be made at least 12 hours in advance or left overnight in the refrigerator, which makes it a good pudding for a dinner party. When you bring it to table in its full elegance of colour, the fresh orange contrasting with the dark chocolate and cream, it is certain to be greeted with admiration, even without 200-year-old plates.

SERVES 6

175g/6oz dark chocolate
90 to 120ml/3 to 4fl oz water
250g/8oz caster sugar
5 large free-range eggs, separated
a little sifted icing sugar for rolling out

FOR THE FILLING:
300ml/10fl oz double cream
grated rind and juice of 1 large orange
icing sugar
fresh orange segments to decorate (optional)

Preheat the oven to 180°C/350°F/gas 4. Line a shallow Swiss roll or roulade tin about 30 × 20cm/12 × 8 inches with oiled baking parchment.

Break the chocolate into pieces and put into a small basin with the water. Put the basin over a saucepan of hot water. Melt the chocolate over a low heat until it forms a thick cream. Remove from the heat.

Put the sugar into a bowl and beat in the egg yolks. Keep beating until the mixture turns lemon in colour. In a separate bowl, whisk the egg whites until they form peaks, rather like firm snow.

Pour the melted chocolate into the egg yolk and sugar mixture and stir well together. Fold the egg whites into the chocolate mixture and pour into the prepared tin. Bake in the preheated oven for 10 to 15 minutes or until the roulade is firm to the touch. Remove from the oven and allow to cool a little, then cover with a clean cloth wrung out in cold water to prevent a sugary crust forming. Leave for at least 12 hours or overnight in a cool place; before leaving overnight, remove the damp cloth and replace with clingfilm.

Lay a piece of baking parchment or greaseproof paper on a worktop and dust with icing sugar. Remove the clingfilm and turn the roulade out upside down on to the icing-sugared paper. Strip off any remaining paper from the roulade.

Make the filling: put the cream into a mixing bowl and add the orange rind and juice. Sprinkle in a little icing sugar to taste and whip until the cream forms soft peaks.

Reserve a little whipped cream for decoration and spread the remainder on to the roulade. Carefully roll up the roulade like a Swiss roll. Put the reserved cream into a piping bag fitted with a star nozzle and pipe the rosettes down the centre of the roulade. Dust with a little more icing sugar, and if desired lay a fresh orange segment on the top of each cream rosette.

Cook's note: Chocolate shavings can be made for decoration if you have the time. Melt chocolate in the usual way, then spread it on a marble work surface and allow to cool. When set, use the edge of a palette knife in a gentle sawing movement to form long thin rolls or shavings of chocolate.

HARVEST ROULADE

During our four-year break from running a restaurant, we ran a small cookery school in Marlborough. Many of our ex-customers came to the school but most of them to ask when we were opening a restaurant again because they were more interested in having Angela cook for them than in learning to cook themselves. We were sufficiently encouraged to open a new Loaves and Fishes restaurant. Angela demonstrated this roulade on the last day of our cookery school. All the students turned out a brilliant roulade and didn't find it as difficult as they first thought it would be. It is a delicious dinner-party pudding, which looks stunning decorated with glowing blackberries and perhaps a late summer rose in the centre. Rolling out the roulade from the baking parchment is not too difficult: do it slowly and carefully and you will succeed. Crème de Mûres is a rich liqueur made from blackberries. It is well worth hunting for in wine merchants but if you cannot find it a miniature of Cassis can be substituted. You can also try out alternative fruit, such as almost any summer or autumn berries, with Kirsch or Grand Marnier as the liqueur.

SERVES 6 to 8

7 free-range eggs, separated
175g/6oz caster sugar
90g/3oz hazelnuts, roasted whole and finely ground
90g/3oz ground almonds
2 teaspoons baking powder
a little sifted icing sugar for rolling out

FOR THE FILLING:
350ml/12fl oz double cream
icing sugar
4 tablespoons Crème de Mûres (blackberry liqueur), or to taste
500g/1lb blackberries

Preheat the oven to 180°C/350°F/gas 4. Line a Swiss roll or roulade tin about 30 × 20cm/12 × 8 inches with oiled baking parchment. Allow at least 5cm/2 inches of parchment beyond the edges of the tray. Grease the parchment lining.

Beat the egg yolks and sugar together in a mixing bowl until thick and creamy. In a separate bowl mix together the ground hazelnuts, ground almonds and baking powder. Fold this into the egg mixture and blend well. Beat the egg whites in a clean bowl until stiff, then fold into the egg and nut mixture. Pour into the prepared tin, gently shaking the mixture into place. Do not spread it with a knife because this destroys the air bubbles and makes the roulade heavy. Bake in the preheated oven for 20 to 25 minutes until firm to the touch.

Remove the roulade from the oven and allow to cool a little. Take a new sheet of baking parchment and sprinkle with sifted icing sugar. Turn the roulade out on to the prepared parchment by inverting the baking tin as close to the paper as possible. Carefully peel off the greased lining parchment, and trim the sides of the roulade if necessary with a sharp knife.

To make the filling: whip the cream and sweeten to taste with icing sugar. Add the blackberry liqueur and blend together until the cream just holds its shape. Spread two-thirds on to the roulade, reserving the remainder for decoration. Sprinkle two-thirds of the blackberries evenly over the cream.

Roll up the roulade from the longest edge. (If you really find rolling up daunting, cut the roulade lengthways into two equal-sized pieces and sandwich together with the fruit and cream in the middle like a gâteau.) Decorate with whirls of the remaining cream and dot the blackberries on top.

WARM RASPBERRY MOUSSE
WITH RHUBARB

I disliked rhubarb intensely as a child, but my mother made me eat it as it was 'good for one's blood'. It was given very little sugar in cooking, and was as bitter, stringy and sour as could be. The same applied to apples. They were never cored properly, and the tough membrane and pips would be left in the pie or stewed fruit for me to encounter. Eating pip casing or core membrane was like eating pieces of fingernail. Young rhubarb should have a sweet taste and tender stalks. Champagne rhubarb is a superb variety. Sweeten with sugar or honey as you wish. You can also add a little preserved ginger to the rhubarb when cooking it but not if it is to accompany this recipe, where the ginger would overpower the raspberry.

SERVES 4 to 6

butter for greasing the dish
60g/2oz butter
90g/3oz caster sugar
3 small free-range eggs, separated
60g/2oz macaroon biscuits, crushed
15g/½oz cornflour
15g/½oz plain flour
125g/4oz raspberries, washed (you can use frozen; remove juice)
250g/8oz rhubarb, washed and cut into small pieces
sugar or clear honey to taste
fresh cream to serve (optional)

Grease a 600ml/1-pint soufflé dish with butter. Grease a piece of baking parchment and line the soufflé dish with it. (Greasing the dish helps the parchment to stick to the sides.)

Cream the butter and 60g/2oz of the sugar together until light, soft and fluffy. Beat the egg yolks into the butter and sugar. Stir in the macaroons, then sift in the cornflour and plain flour. Blend all the ingredients well together, then stir in the raspberries.

Whisk the egg whites until stiff and beat in the remaining 30g/1oz sugar. Fold into the raspberry mixture. When everything is well blended, pour into the prepared soufflé dish. Cover tightly with kitchen foil and steam for a good hour until firm and set.

While the mousse is steaming, put the rhubarb into a saucepan along with a little water, add sugar or honey to taste, and cook until the rhubarb is soft. Drain and put into a warm serving dish. Sprinkle a little more sugar on top or drizzle a little honey over.

Remove the mousse from the steamer, place a plate over the dish and turn out. Peel away the parchment. Serve with the rhubarb, and a little pouring cream if desired.

FRESH RASPBERRY TORTE

We made this delicious pudding during our outside catering days for the late John Betjeman's seventieth birthday. He was staying with his daughter Candida Lycett Green at her home in Wiltshire. It was a wonderful, homely occasion. Dinner was held in the nursery, and at the conclusion of dinner a guest played the piano and everyone joined in for a song or a poem. When we had completed the clearing-up, which we did very slowly, we did not really want to leave. The secret of this flan is in the shortbread pastry. It is well worth the little extra effort it takes. You need a food processor, and the measurements for the ingredients must be exact. Angela has tried to round up or down the measures but the pastry does not work so well, so we apologize for the delicacy required in obtaining the measure of half an egg white; the other half can be returned to the yolk and used to brush over the pastry if desired. The filling is very easy but the flan cases must not be filled too long before required or the pastry will absorb the moisture from the cream and fruit and become soggy.

MAKES 2 FLANS

FOR THE PASTRY:
250g/9oz plain flour
200g/(scant) 7oz English dairy butter
75g/2½oz caster sugar
finely grated rind of 1 lemon
½ free-range egg white

FOR THE FILLING:
600ml/1 pint thick double cream
1 miniature bottle (120ml/4fl oz) Kirsch
caster sugar to taste
1lb/500g fresh raspberries (or strawberries if preferred)
icing sugar for dusting

First make the pastry: put the flour into a food processor. Cut the butter into small pieces and add to the flour. Mix until the butter is well blended in and there are no lumps. Put in the sugar and lemon rind and mix again. Add the egg white, and mix once more until a firm dough has formed.

Dust a worktop lightly with flour – not too much or the pastry will lose its shortness. Remove the dough from the food processor and divide into 2 equal pieces. Roll out one piece of pastry fairly thinly and line a 25cm/10-inch loose-bottomed flan tin with it. Trim off any pastry hanging over the edge. Repeat the process with the second piece of pastry. Allow the flan cases to chill in the top of the refrigerator or in the freezer for 10 minutes to make the dough firm. (The flan cases can be frozen at this stage and cooked straight from the freezer.)

Preheat the oven to 190°C/375°F/gas 5. Remove the flan cases from the refrigerator or freezer and bake until a very light biscuit colour: the colour of shortbread.

Then make the filling: whisk the cream until it just begins to thicken, then gradually add the Kirsch, whisking as you go. Add a little caster sugar to taste (it brings out the flavour of the Kirsch and fruit). Divide the flavoured cream between the flan cases. Place the raspberries in circles on top of the cream, top side up. If strawberries are used, slice them and arrange the slices in circles, overlapping each other. (Use a mixture of both fruits if desired.) Dust lightly with icing sugar and serve.

LIME AND LEMON
CURD TARTLETS

Mondays are our only day off, so this is the time that we entertain, usually very informally in the restaurant's kitchen. We have a friend who spends half his time in England and the other half in France. He loves classic cars and usually turns up for supper parties in one of his collection of them. The last time he and his wife came to supper this tartlet was the sweet course, and, on the promise that this pudding would be on the menu, he and 32 other classic-car owners are to come to Sunday lunch conveyed in a vintage coach. The great thing about this recipe is that you make the curd and put it into jars to be used as and when required, such as spreading on scones or toast. You need only half the quantity to make these tartlets.

MAKES 500 G/1 LB, HALF OF WHICH IS USED FOR
4 TO 6 TARTLETS

FOR THE CURD:
125g/4oz unsalted butter
grated rind and juice of 3 limes
grated rind and juice of 1 lemon
3 large free-range eggs
250g/8oz caster sugar

FOR THE TARTLETS:
250g/8oz shortbread pastry (see page 196: Fresh Raspberry Torte)
4 to 6 apricots

Put all the ingredients for the curd into a basin and stand over a saucepan of hot water, making sure the water is not touching the basin. Whisk continuously over a low heat until all the ingredients are liquid. Continue whisking until the mixture thickens into a curd. This can take a bit of time so make it with a friend's help if you can. Remove the curd from the heat and pour into 2 × 250g/8oz clean jars. Cover in the usual way and store in the refrigerator until required.

Roll out the pastry into circles to line 4 to 6 12cm/5-inch flan tins. Press a pastry circle into each tin, and trim the edges if necessary. Chill the flan cases in the refrigerator or freezer for 10 minutes to firm the pastry.

Preheat the oven to 190°C/375°F/gas 5.

Remove the flan cases from the refrigerator or freezer and bake briefly in the preheated oven until only just turning a light shortbread colour. Allow to cool.

Spoon the curd into the baked and cooled cases. Slice the apricots thinly, arrange over the curd in the flan cases, and serve.

SHERRY AND ALMOND CREAM MERINGUES

As an Officers' Steward in the Women's Royal Naval Service many years ago I was stationed at HMS *Raleigh* in Devon, and early one morning was dispatched along with four other members of the same watch to Dartmoor to await the arrival of the First Sea Lord. He was visiting a group of sea cadets and midshipmen taking part in a military exercise on the moor. I waited for the admiral's helicopter dressed in a far too big, white, submariner's jersey and black seaboots, and holding a silver salver that held tiny sherry glasses. We served lunch in an old Nissen hut, and it was silver service too, with EPNS vegetable tureens and wardroom china, all washed up afterwards in a gravel stream that meandered close by. It was certainly a change from being in the wardroom. This recipe is an alternative way of serving sherry if standing around on a windy moor with a silver salver is not your style. Remember, when making meringues, that they dry out rather than cook, so long exposure to gentle heat is the secret.

MAKES 4 MERINGUES (8 CIRCLES)

175g/6oz caster sugar
90g/3oz ground almonds
3 free-range egg whites

FOR THE FILLING:
300ml/10fl oz double cream
90ml/3fl oz well-flavoured dark cream sherry
a little icing sugar to taste (optional)
a little sifted icing sugar and 60g/2oz flaked toasted almonds for decoration
fresh cream or fruit sauce of your choice to serve

Preheat the oven to 160°C/325°F/gas 3.

Mix the sugar and ground almonds together in a bowl, pressing out any lumps. Whisk the egg whites in a separate bowl until stiff (the eggs, not your arms). You should be able to turn the bowl upside down without the egg whites falling out. Carefully fold the sugar and almonds into the egg whites.

Line 2 baking sheets with baking parchment paper. Use a spoon to make 8 equal circles of meringue on the paper. Dry out the meringues in the preheated oven for 1 hour. Check after 40 to 45 minutes that they are not browning too quickly. If they are, lower the heat slightly. The thinner the meringue circles, the quicker they will dry out, though circles spread out too thinly will be difficult to handle. The meringues should be a pale golden-brown.

Remove the meringues from the oven and place on a wire rack, peeling off the parchment carefully. Allow to cool.

To make the filling: whisk the double cream until it just holds its shape. Gradually pour in the sherry, whisking as you go. Add icing sugar to taste if desired. When all the sherry has been incorporated and the cream is holding its shape, divide the cream evenly among 4 of the meringue circles. Sandwich together with the remaining 4 circles. Dust with the sifted icing sugar, scatter over the flaked, toasted almonds and serve with fresh cream or a fruit sauce of your choice.

FRUITY ALMOND CREAMS

For centuries most people kept at least one house cow. Town folk who could not keep their own dairy cow would have their milk delivered in wooden (later metal) churns. Milkmaids in London sold milk in wooden pails hanging from their shoulders on a wooden yoke. There were even cow keepers in Hyde Park. In many towns dairy cows were kept at the back of a shop and the milk ladled from churns. I remember being given, at the age of twelve, milk after it had been through the cooler straight from the cow. It was the most delicious drink I have ever had. I wish we could do the same today. Our milk is so insipid now. Creams and cheeses taste bland and go off quickly in their packages. The friendly bacteria, essential in the making of traditional thick cream and mature cheeses, have been boiled out. Shrink-wrapped wedges of cheese – it hardly warrants the name – are in the shops before the cheese has had a chance to ripen. England's heritage, traditional milking and cheese-making, is almost a thing of the past. If you can find a source of unpasteurized cream and cheeses you will find it makes all the difference to the flavour and the goodness of a dish. Enterprising cheese-makers and dairy farmers are making a great effort to bring back the traditional foods of England. The more we can support them, the better able they will be to give us real food at competitive prices. This is a very simple pudding to make, and ideal for children wanting to have a go at 'cooking' for the first time. It is also nutritious with its double cream, fruit and honey.

SERVES 4

2 bananas, peeled and thinly sliced
2 fresh ripe pears, peeled, cored and chopped
125g/4oz raisins
juice of 1 lemon
225ml/8fl oz double cream (unpasteurized if you can get it)
60g/2oz slivered almonds
2 tablespoons clear honey
extra almonds or raisins to decorate

Put the banana, pear and raisins into a mixing bowl. Cut the lemon in half and squeeze the juice over the fruit.

Pour the cream into a basin and whisk until it becomes quite stiff. Sprinkle the almonds into the whipped cream and stir in the honey. Mix thoroughly until well blended. Add the chopped fruit and lemon juice to the cream and honey mixture and stir well in. Spoon the fruit and almond cream into glass bowls. Chill in the refrigerator before serving.

When ready to serve, sprinkle the tops of the creams with chopped almonds or raisins.

ICED STRAWBERRY SEMI-FREDDO

This is a semi-frozen mousse with a closer texture than an ordinary mousse. A variety of fruit purées can be used – an excellent way of using and freezing any glut of fruit you may have. The semi-freddo can be served in one large glass serving bowl or individual ramekins. Make it a day in advance.

SERVES 6 to 8

500g / 1lb strawberries
4 free-range egg yolks
250g / 8oz sugar
4 tablespoons water
juice of ½ lemon
300ml / 10fl oz double cream
1 miniature bottle (120ml / 4fl oz) Cointreau or Grand Marnier

Purée the strawberries; they should make a little over 300ml/ 10fl oz. Strain the purée if you don't like pips. Pour into a large bowl and set aside.

Put the egg yolks and sugar into a basin and beat well together. Add the water and lemon juice and continue beating until the mixture is creamy and thick. Place the basin over a saucepan of simmering water and continue beating until the yolks begin to thicken slightly. Stand the basin in cold water and continue to beat until the mixture is cold. The mixture will thicken and increase in bulk as you do so.

Whip the double cream until firm, stir in the liqueur and fold lightly into the strawberry purée. Add the egg yolk and sugar mixture, folding in lightly. Pour into your chosen serving dish(es) and freeze overnight.

Remove from the freezer and transfer to the refrigerator about 1 hour before serving if using a large serving bowl; 20 minutes before if using individual ramekin dishes.

ELDERFLOWER AND ROSE PETAL SORBET

The ingredients for this recipe provide a lovely blend of early summer aromas. Angela's mother, who tested this recipe for us, telephoned from the Dordogne area of France to say that she could not bear to pick the petals off her beautiful roses. All is well, however – the petals are picked from full-blown roses just before they fall off. A good-scented rose is essential for this recipe. We have found that red roses are one of the best: they give a strong scent and a beautiful pink colour to the sorbet. Make the sorbet a day before you need it to allow it to freeze overnight.

SERVES 6

450ml/15fl oz water
300g/10oz caster sugar
thinly pared and juice rind of 2 lemons
1.1 litres/2 pints freshly picked elderflowers, stalks removed
1.1 litres/2 pints freshly picked rose petals
4 tablespoons triple-strength rose water
rose petals and elderflowers to decorate

Put the water, sugar, lemon rind and juice into a saucepan. Heat gently until the sugar has dissolved. Remove from the heat.

Steep the elderflowers and rose petals in the sugar syrup until the syrup is cold. Strain through muslin into a bowl. Discard the elderflowers and rose petals and stir the rose water into the liquid. Freeze overnight in a suitable container.

Remove the sorbet from the freezer about 20 minutes before serving. To serve: use a spoon to scrape the sorbet out of the container into a light snow which you pile into serving glasses. Decorate with fresh rose petals and/or a small sprig of elderflowers.

PINK CHAMPAGNE, POMEGRANATE AND PINK GRAPEFRUIT SORBET

A very special sorbet that we make for Christmas Eve dinner. Good rosé wine can be substituted for pink champagne if you prefer. The remaining champagne or rosé can be drunk with the sorbet – if there is any left over, of course. Pour a little pink champagne or wine over the completed sorbet just before serving, scatter a few pomegranate seeds over, place a sprig of holly on top and you have a refreshing, romantic, festive sweet. Make the sorbet a day before you need it to allow it to freeze overnight.

SERVES 6 to 8

150ml/5fl oz pink champagne or rosé wine
350g/12oz caster sugar
juice of 2 pink grapefruit
juice of 1 lemon
6 pomegranates (1 for decoration)

Put the champagne or rosé wine and the sugar into a saucepan over a low heat and dissolve the sugar. Increase the heat and boil the liquid until you have a sugar syrup. This will happen quickly so do not leave the pan at this stage.

Remove from the heat and add the grapefruit and lemon juices. Cut 5 pomegranates in half and squeeze the juice through a sieve into the sugar syrup. Blend the juices and syrup well together. Pour the mixture into a suitable container, allow to cool, then freeze overnight.

Remove the sorbet from the freezer about 20 minutes before serving. Take the remaining pomegranate, cut away the skin and carefully remove the membrane, pulling away the seeds.

To serve: use a spoon to scrape the sorbet out of the container into a light snow which you pile into the centre of a pretty plate. Scatter a few loose pomegranate seeds over the top, place a sprig of holly in the centre and pour over a little champagne or rosé wine.

You can serve the sorbet in glasses if you prefer. If you do, you will not need so many pomegranate seeds. You could also serve with segments of pink grapefruit instead of (or as well as) the pomegranate.

HONEY AND GINGER ICE CREAM

Honey is one of the oldest forms of sweetener and was used when sugar was rare and expensive. Ancient civilizations thought honey had life-enhancing properties and consumed it in a variety of dishes and drinks. We make no apology for using ginger again: it is a marvellous ingredient. It gives a spicy and oriental flavour to dishes that may otherwise be ordinary. Not that homemade ice cream is ordinary – it is a special treat, to which bought ice cream bears no resemblance whatsoever. It is easy to make, and you need only a mixing bowl, a metal spoon and a freezer. Leave the spoon in the mixture while it is in the freezer and it will freeze much more quickly, but remove the spoon before the ice cream is completely frozen. The basis of this ice cream is the making of a honey and ginger custard. More honey and ginger can be added according to your individual taste. Serve with brandy snaps, on its own, or with an apple or pear pie, or pile into halves of fresh pear with a little ginger preserve syrup poured over the top. Make the ice cream a day before you need it to allow it to freeze overnight.

SERVES 6 to 8

2 tablespoons cornflour, slackened with a little water
450ml/15fl oz full-cream milk
3 free-range egg yolks
60g/2oz caster sugar
2 tablespoons preserved ginger, finely chopped
4 tablespoons preserved ginger syrup
120ml/4fl oz clear honey
juice of 2 lemons
450ml/15fl oz double cream

Blend the slackened cornflour with a little of the milk until smooth and creamy. Beat the egg yolks with the caster sugar until thick and pale.

Heat the milk in a saucepan and blend in the slackened cornflour. Cook until it has thickened, stirring all the time to prevent any lumps from forming. When thick, pour into the egg yolk and sugar mixture. Whisk well until all the ingredients are thoroughly blended. Add the ginger, ginger syrup, honey and lemon juice and stir well. Transfer the mixture to a clean saucepan and stir over a low heat for a couple of minutes to cook the egg yolks. Do not boil. Remove from the heat, pour into a large bowl and allow to cool. Press a piece of greaseproof paper over the surface of the custard to prevent a skin from forming; stir from time to time.

When the mixture is cold, whisk the double cream until it just holds its shape and fold into the honey and ginger custard, using a metal spoon. Blend well together, pour into a container and freeze overnight. There is no need to beat it during freezing. Remove from the freezer 30 minutes before serving.

7

Cakes, Bread and Pastry

LOAVES AND FISHES
CHOCOLATE FUDGE

Always served with the coffee, this delicious fudge is sweet but not sickly. We have to make quite large quantities as it is eaten quickly, and not only by our guests. You will need a sugar thermometer; most cook shops have them in stock if you don't already have one. A Swiss roll tin is ideal for setting the fudge: the sides of the tin help to stop the fudge mixture from spreading over the edge. You will also need a large, heavy-based saucepan for making it.

MAKES 1.25 KG / 2½ LB FUDGE

300ml/10fl oz full-cream milk
1kg/2lb unrefined granulated sugar
125g/4oz butter
2 tablespoons clear honey
250g/8oz dark chocolate

Put all the ingredients except the chocolate into the heavy-based saucepan. Dissolve the sugar over a medium heat, then bring to the boil stirring from time to time. Place a sugar thermometer in the mixture and boil until it reaches 120°C/240°F. Remove from the heat, add the chocolate, and stir until the chocolate has melted. Beat the mixture well to blend the chocolate and to allow air into the fudge. The mixture will become lighter in colour. Pour into the Swiss roll tin and smooth with a palette knife as it begins to set. Mark with a knife into squares.

Allow to set completely, turn out of the tin and break into squares. Any tiny pieces of fudge left over can be saved and served over ice cream. Store in an airtight container in a cool place, not the refrigerator (where it goes damp).

EASTER ALMOND CHERRY CAKE

It was Easter Monday, stormy and wet, and we were the proud owners of one small canal boat, flat at both ends, the type that is called a pram. We named it Sloe. We puttered down the canal from Pewsey Wharf towards Devizes, but were being blown about by strong winds. About 10 minutes into our journey the motor spluttered and lapsed into an indifferent silence. It was never to go again despite all our efforts at pulling the cord, efforts which finally propelled Angela backwards into the cabin when the cord snapped. Out came the oars, which we poked through the small windows, and we began to row. After much circling and bank buffeting we did manage to reach a mooring, a small, almost rotten wooden post in the bank, surrounded by stinging nettles. The 'commodore' of the wharf came along to ask if we wanted help. 'Certainly not,' I replied. 'We have been in the Women's Royal Naval Service, you know.' We managed to secure the boat and went home to tea, soaked to the skin. Fortunately, Angela had made this cake a couple of days before (it needs to be kept for at least a day before eating). And what happened to Sloe? We gave her to the local sea cadets for training.

MAKES 1 × 20 CM/8 INCH CAKE

butter for greasing the tin
125g/4oz butter
125g/4oz vanilla or caster sugar
2 free-range eggs, beaten
grated rind and juice of 1 small lemon
125g/4oz plain flour
½ teaspoon baking powder
60g/2oz ground almonds
60g/2oz blanched sliced almonds
500g/1lb whole unbleached glacé cherries (not the bright red ones)
icing sugar to finish

FOR THE ALMOND PASTE:
90g/3oz ground almonds
45g/1½ oz caster sugar
45g/1½ oz icing sugar
1 small free-range egg, beaten

Preheat the oven to 150°C/300°F/gas 2. Grease a 20cm/8-inch round, loose-bottomed cake tin with butter and line with baking parchment.

First make the almond paste: put the ground almonds and caster sugar into a mixing bowl. Sift in the icing sugar. Mix together. Pour in a little of the beaten egg and bind into a stiff paste. Add a little more egg if necessary to form a workable but not too soft paste; you may not need to use all the beaten egg. Turn the paste out on to a board that has been lightly dusted with icing sugar and roll out into a 20cm/8-inch circle, the size of the cake tin.

Then make the cake: cream the butter and sugar together in a mixing bowl. Gradually add half the eggs, beating as you go. Add the lemon rind and juice. Sift the flour and baking powder together and fold this into the butter and sugar mixture along with the remaining egg. Fold in the ground and sliced almonds and finally the cherries, then blend all the ingredients well together.

Spread half the cake mixture in the bottom of the prepared tin. Place the circle of almond paste on top, pressing gently into place. Cover the paste evenly with the remaining cake mixture and bake in the preheated oven for 3 hours until firm to the touch. Remove from the oven, loosen the sides of the tin, transfer the cake to a wire tray and allow to cool. Keep for at least a day before eating. To finish, sift over a little icing sugar.

CONNEMARA CHOCOLATE CAKE

One year on St Patrick's Day, 17 March, we devised a special menu with an Irish flavour: Emerald Isle spinach roulade, Skebawn smoked salmon cheesecake, Guinness casserole, roast lamb Curranhilty, St Patrick's Irish coffee ice-cream, and this chocolate cake, which we served with cream flavoured with Irish coffee. This recipe is for two cakes, which you can sandwich together if you like with double cream or chocolate buttercream.

MAKES 2 × 20 CM/8 INCH CAKES

butter for greasing the tins
125g/4oz vegetable fat (shortening)
300g/10oz caster sugar
60g/2oz dark chocolate, broken into pieces
200ml/7fl oz water
30g/1oz cocoa powder
175g/6oz plain flour
¼ teaspoon baking powder
1 teaspoon bicarbonate of soda
2 free-range eggs, beaten

FOR THE ICING:
125g/4oz sifted icing sugar
2 teaspoons cocoa powder, mixed with 4 tablespoons warm water

Preheat the oven to 180°C/350°F/gas 4. Grease 2 × 20cm/8-inch diameter sandwich tins and line with baking parchment.

Cream together the vegetable fat and sugar until the mixture is light and fluffy.

Put the pieces of chocolate into a saucepan, add the water and dissolve over a low heat. When the chocolate has melted, whisk in the cocoa powder until thoroughly blended and lump-free. Remove from the heat and allow to cool.

Sift the flour, baking powder and bicarbonate of soda into a mixing bowl.

Whisk the beaten egg into the sugar and fat mixture. Fold in the flour, a little at a time, alternating with the melted chocolate. Blend well together so that there are no dry patches. Divide the mixture evenly between the prepared sandwich tins and bake in the preheated oven for 35 minutes until springy to the touch. Remove from the oven and allow to cool slightly before removing from the tins and placing on a wire rack to cool completely.

Prepare the icing by mixing the ingredients together until smooth. Spread evenly over the top of the cold cakes.

DARK TREACLE
GINGERBREAD CAKE

Many years ago, we were asked to tea by a retired major and his wife who lived at that time in a large country house with racing stables attached. The major had a reputation for plain speaking and prompt action. He would rake level the gravel at the front of the house and, should any unfortunate drive upon it, would bring his stick smartly down on the bonnet of the car, until the car backed off and parked at the side of the house on the tarmac. For tea we sat by the fire and had a wonderful dark, sticky, rich gingerbread cake. When we make our gingerbread cake, it brings back memories of that wonderful character, the huge fire, and being waited upon for a change. This cake keeps well for a long time, if you are able to resist it. Serve with cream for a winter dinner party. Such a rich cake tends to sink in the middle during cooking. Do not worry, this is quite usual and does not harm it. You need a deep, 18 to 20cm/7 to 8-inch long loaf tin. If the tin is too shallow, the mixture will spill over the rim during baking.

MAKES 6 to 8 LARGE SLICES OR 12 to 14 THINNER ONES

butter for greasing the tin
125g/4oz dark Barbados sugar
125g/4oz butter
150g/5oz black treacle
150g/5oz golden syrup
2 free-range eggs
125g/4oz plain flour
125g/4oz wholemeal flour
3 teaspoons ground ginger
60g/2oz preserved ginger, finely chopped
60g/2oz sultanas
½ teaspoon bicarbonate soda
4 tablespoons warm milk

Preheat the oven to 160°C/325°F/gas 3. Grease the loaf tin (see introduction to recipe) with butter and line with baking parchment.

Cream the sugar and butter together. Stir in the treacle, syrup and eggs. Sift the two flours and ground ginger together, then tip into the butter and sugar mixture. Stir in the ginger pieces and sultanas. Finally, stir the bicarbonate of soda into the warmed milk, and pour into the cake mixture. Make sure all the ingredients are well blended, then pour into the prepared loaf tin. Bake in the preheated oven for 1½ hours. If you prefer a cake that is less sticky, bake for a further 15 to 20 minutes.

DATE AND WALNUT YOGHURT CAKE

1981 saw the Loaves and Fishes move from Wootton Bassett to Rockley Chapel. We did most of the groundwork ourselves. One job was to clear the overgrown drive and car park leading to the chapel. It seemed to take for ever, but at the end of each afternoon Angela or our dear friend from Pond Cottage would supply tea and cake. This cake is an old favourite, and brings back memories of digging, painting, plastering and the odd bit of wood planing. The cake will benefit from the fruit having a lengthy soak. Put the dates and raisins in a saucepan with the apple juice, heat gently for a few minutes, then leave to soak overnight in the juice. The cake will absorb the liquid and become more plump. If you do not have time, however, the cake will still be fine without the overnight soaking. This is a moist, close-textured cake, perfect for tea.

MAKES 1 × 20CM/8 INCH CAKE

butter for greasing the tin
250g/8oz dates, stoned and roughly chopped
90g/3oz raisins
150ml/5fl oz apple juice
120ml/4fl oz clear honey or golden syrup
120ml/4fl oz vegetable oil
2 large free-range eggs, beaten
90g/3oz plain white flour
90g/3oz wholemeal flour
½ teaspoon bicarbonate of soda
2 teaspoons ground mixed spice
150ml/5fl oz natural yoghurt
90g/3oz chopped walnuts

Preheat the oven to 180°C/350°F/gas 4. Grease a deep 20cm/8-inch loose-sided round cake tin with butter and line with baking parchment.

If you have not soaked the fruit overnight (see introduction), put the dates and raisins into a saucepan, pour in the apple juice and heat gently for a few minutes until the fruit is nicely plump. Remove from the heat and allow to cool.

Put the honey or syrup, oil, egg, both flours, bicarbonate of soda, mixed spice and yoghurt into a food processor. Blend thoroughly until you have a thick batter. Pour the batter into a mixing bowl and add the walnuts, soaked fruit and apple juice. Blend well together.

Pour the mixture into the prepared cake tin and bake on the top shelf of the preheated oven for 1 hour, or a little longer, depending on the temperament of your cooker.

PEACH AND ALMOND CAKE

A great favourite with cake-lovers and pudding-eaters alike. Serve with flavoured cream as a sweet course, or as a cake for tea or supper with a glass of Australian Muscat (a wonderful drink that tastes like liquid Christmas pudding). Ripe peaches are a must for this cake and, ideally, the apricot jam should be homemade. We flavour sweetened whipped cream with a few drops of Archer's peach liqueur or Kirsch to serve with the cake.

MAKES 1 × 20 CM/8 INCH CAKE

melted butter for greasing the tin
500g/1lb ripe but firm peaches, stones removed, skinned
juice of ½ lemon
150g/5oz plain flour
good pinch of salt
1½ level teaspoons baking powder
75g/2½ oz caster sugar
60g/2oz butter, melted
2 large free-range eggs, beaten
4 tablespoons Kirsch
60g/2oz lightly toasted almonds

FOR THE GLAZE:
2 tablespoons apricot jam
4 tablespoons water
splash of Kirsch

Preheat the oven to 180°C/350°F/gas 4. Line a 20cm/8-inch cake tin with baking parchment and brush with melted butter.

Cut the peaches into pieces and put into a bowl with the lemon juice. Turn the pieces in the juice so the peach does not discolour.

Sift the flour, salt and baking powder into a separate bowl. Stir in the sugar and make a well in the centre. Pour in the melted butter, eggs and Kirsch. Blend all the ingredients well together. Fold in the almonds and peaches.

Pour the mixture into the prepared cake tin and bake for about 1 hour until cooked through and firm to the touch. If after the first 30 minutes of cooking the top of the cake is browning well, lower the oven temperature by a few degrees for the remaining 30 minutes.

Make the glaze by simmering together the apricot jam, water and Kirsch. Sieve out any lumps. Remove the cake from the oven and allow to cool. Remove the cake from the tin, carefully peel away the lining paper and brush the cake with apricot glaze.

BANANA AND
PINE KERNEL CAKE

This is another of our Monday, day-off recipes. Angela found some very ripe bananas in the larder and set to work to see what she could make with them. This rather unusual cake was the result. Though a tea-time cake, it is not over-sweet and has a buttery, brioche-like texture, so it can accompany savoury salads and meat pâtés. Over-ripe bananas give a good, strong flavour to the cake.

MAKES 1 × 750 G / 1½ LB CAKE OR 2 SMALLER ONES

2 tablespoons cream cheese
2 ripe bananas, peeled
grated rind and juice of 1 small lemon
175g / 6oz self-raising flour
½ teaspoon bicarbonate of soda
½ teaspoon ground cinnamon
¼ teaspoon sea salt
150g / 5oz caster sugar
90g / 3oz butter
1 large free-range egg, beaten
90g / 3oz pine kernels

Preheat the oven to 180°C/350°F/gas 4. Line a 750g/1½lb loaf tin (or 2 smaller ones) with baking parchment.

Using a fork, mash the cream cheese, banana and lemon rind and juice together in a bowl until the mixture is smooth and lump-free.

Sift the flour, bicarbonate of soda, cinnamon and salt into a bowl.

In a separate mixing bowl cream the sugar and butter together until light and fluffy. Add the beaten egg a little at a time, beating as you go. Put a tablespoon of the banana purée into the creamed sugar and butter mixture, add a tablespoon of the sifted dry ingredients, and cut and fold in. Repeat the process until the all ingredients are used up. Fold in the pine kernels, pour the mixture into the prepared loaf tin and bake in the preheated oven for about 45 minutes until golden-brown. (Smaller cakes cook more quickly.) Test the cake by inserting a skewer in the centre. If it comes away clean, the cake is done. If the cake is getting too brown on top and is still not cooked in the centre, lower the heat and place a little kitchen foil over the top to prevent further browning.

Remove from the oven, leave to cool in the tin(s) for a few minutes, then turn on to a wire rack, carefully peel off the lining parchment and leave to cool completely.

HONEY AND
PECAN NUT MUFFINS

A few years ago we were in Paris. Our first meal in the hotel, on arriving at nine o'clock on Sunday evening, was chicken and chips, burnt. The grand hotel, full of marble, mirrors and chambermaids in black and white lace, was very close to the opera house, and the low standard of food came as a great surprise. Breakfast was even more dismal: dried-up croissants, rock-hard muffins and packet jam. We left the hotel and had a marvellous breakfast in a brasserie a little way along the boulevard. These honey muffins will not be around long enough to go as hard as those from the hotel. They make a pleasant change for breakfast. Pull the cooked muffins apart when buttering them; a knife compresses them and makes them soggy.

MAKES 24

butter for greasing the tins
250g/8oz plain flour
2 teaspoons baking powder
1 teaspoon cream of tartar
60g/2oz caster sugar
½ teaspoon salt
2 small free-range eggs, beaten
60g/2oz butter, melted
4 tablespoons clear honey
150ml/5fl oz milk
60g/2oz sultanas
90g/3oz pecan nuts, broken into small pieces

Preheat the oven to 200°C/400°F/gas 6. Grease 2 muffin or cake tins, each of which holds 12.

Sift together the flour, baking powder, cream of tartar, sugar and salt into a large mixing bowl. Stir in the egg, butter, honey and a quarter of the milk. Stir together gently. Add the sultanas and pecan nut pieces. Pour in the remaining milk and blend the ingredients well together. Fill the tins two-thirds full and bake in the preheated oven for 20 to 25 minutes.

Allow the muffins to cool slightly in the tins before removing. They will come away from the tin more easily that way. Serve immediately with dairy butter, jam or marmalade.

BRANDY SNAPS

Vanilla is the more usual ingredient for brandy snaps, but we like to use brandy. What is a brandy snap without brandy? In this recipe, however, the choice is yours. Use a thick baking tray if you can. The snaps will take longer to cook, but they will also keep warm for longer, giving you time to work them into shape. Take care not to over-brown the brandy snaps when cooking or they will become inedible.

MAKES 18 to 20

butter for greasing the tray
125g/4oz unsalted butter
125g/4oz demerara sugar
125g/4oz golden syrup
125g/4oz plain flour
pinch of salt
1 teaspoon ground ginger
2 to 3 drops vanilla extract or 2 teaspoons brandy
1 teaspoon lemon juice
300ml/10fl oz double cream to fill the snaps

Preheat the oven to 160°C/325°F/gas 3. Grease a thick baking tray with butter.

Put the butter, sugar and syrup into a saucepan and heat gently until the butter has melted and the sugar dissolved. Remove from the heat and allow to cool. You can speed up the cooling process by standing the saucepan in a bowl of cold water for a minute or two.

Sift the flour with the salt and ginger into the melted butter and sugar mixture. Blend together, then add the vanilla extract or brandy and the lemon juice, and stir well.

Put teaspoons of the mixture on to the prepared baking tray, about 10cm/4 inches apart. Bake in the preheated oven for about

8 minutes. Remove from the oven and allow the biscuits to cool slightly before handling.

Take a palette knife or fish slice and slide it under each brandy snap, turn it over and roll it around the handle of a wooden spoon. Allow each snap to cool briefly on the spoon handle before setting it aside to cool completely. If you have enough wooden spoons, allow the snaps to cool completely on the spoon handles.

As soon as the snaps are cold, store in an airtight tin. When required, whip the double cream (flavoured with vanilla extract or any flavouring of your choice) and spoon or pipe into the brandy snaps.

YORKSHIRE TEACAKES

During our outside catering days, when we were not working we would take a trip to the south coast and have a picnic on the shingle. We would toast these teacakes on open driftwood fires, and they tasted fabulous. They also taste good toasted under the grill, spread with lots of butter and eaten at the kitchen table or by the fireside.

MAKES 8 to 10

500g/1lb strong white flour
250g/8oz plain white flour
¼ teaspoon salt
90g/3oz caster sugar
1 sachet (7g/¼oz) fast-action dried yeast
60g/2oz lard
¼ nutmeg, freshly grated
125g/4oz currants
60g/2oz piece crystallized lemon peel, very finely chopped
300ml/10fl oz warm milk
150ml/5fl oz hot water

Sift the two flours, salt and sugar together into a mixing bowl. Stir in the yeast. Using your fingers, rub in the lard. This can be done in a food processor if preferred. Add the nutmeg, currants and lemon peel. Mix well together. Make a well in the centre of the mixture. Mix the milk and water together and pour into the well a little at a time, mixing as you go. Keep adding until you have a nice firm dough mixture: you may not need all the liquid. Knead lightly, then leave in a warm place to prove and double in size.

Once the dough has risen, form into 8 or 10 bun shapes. Knead each dough piece until the mixture is smooth by bringing the sides to the middle and turning around and repeating until the dough is smooth. Place the kneaded buns on a greased baking tray.

Allow a little space around each bun for expansion. Leave to rise until slightly puffy: around 15 minutes in a warm kitchen. Preheat the oven to 220°C/425°F/gas 7.

Bake the risen teacakes in the preheated oven for 30 minutes. For a flat top, turn them over 5 minutes before the end of cooking time. Transfer to a wire rack and allow to cool slightly before pulling apart and spreading with butter (never cut a freshly baked teacake as this makes it stodgy). For cold teacakes, cut each bun in half, and toast before eating.

PECAN NUT FLAPJACKS

Angela's favourite meal is tea-time, which explains why she is forever making cakes, biscuits or flapjacks. These pecan nut flapjacks are quite delicious but will not last long when friends drop in for tea or coffee. If you wish to keep a store, double the quantity and hide some in a tin for a couple of days. Walnuts can be used instead of pecan nuts if preferred.

MAKES 16 × 5 CM/2 INCH SQUARE FLAPJACKS

60g/2oz butter
60g/2oz light soft brown sugar
4 tablespoons golden syrup
150g/5oz rolled oats
90g/3oz pecan nuts, broken into small pieces

Preheat the oven to 180°C/350°F/gas 4.

Melt the butter in a saucepan, making sure it does not brown. Pour in the sugar and the syrup. Stir, then remove from the heat. Add the oats and pecan nuts, and mix thoroughly to distribute them evenly through the mixture.

Press the mixture into a shallow, 20cm/8-inch square baking tin. Press any protruding nuts well down into the tin to prevent scorching. Bake for 20 to 25 minutes until soft in texture and golden in colour. Do not over-brown the flapjacks or they will spoil.

Remove the flapjacks from the oven and allow to cool a little and set. While the mixture is still slightly warm, mark with a knife into squares or fingers. Allow to cool completely, then turn out and store in a suitable container until required.

SULTANA SCONES

One of the things that Angela loves about tea-time is the sound of china clinking together, reminding her of when she was six, and allowed to make scones and cakes in her grandmother's kitchen and then wheel them out into the garden on a large wooden trolley with the tea service merrily tinkling away.

MAKES 8

500g/1lb self-raising flour
½ teaspoon salt
90g/3oz margarine
60g/2oz caster sugar
125g/4oz sultanas
2 small free-range eggs, beaten
150ml/5fl oz fromage frais
a little milk for mixing

Preheat the oven to 230°C/450°F/gas 8.

Put the flour and salt into a mixing bowl and blend together. Rub in the margarine and stir in the sugar and sultanas. Add the eggs, fromage frais and a little drop of milk, and bind the ingredients together to form a firm but soft dough. Add a little more milk if needed.

Roll out the dough on a floured board. Do not roll out too thinly, the aim is to have a fairly deep scone. Cut into circles about 5cm/2 inches in diameter. Push any protruding sultanas well into the dough to prevent them from burning. Bake at the top of the preheated oven for 10 to 12 minutes until well risen and golden. Allow to cool on a wire rack. Best served warm with clotted or double cream, but equally delicious on their own. Remember to pull the scones apart. The dough will compress into a stodge if cut with a knife.

WHOLEMEAL BREAD

We bake all our own bread using organically grown wholemeal stoneground flour, which is entirely free from fertilizers and chemicals. We buy it in 32kg sacks direct from Dove's Farm just down the road near Hungerford. The flour can be bought in smaller bags from good health-food stores and supermarkets. Using natural flour gives the bread a nutty flavour. Served hot from the oven, it is a great favourite with our restaurant guests, and a real diet-defeater. It also makes excellent toast for breakfast. All other mass-produced, so-called bread pales into insignificance next to your own homemade bread.

MAKES 3 LOAVES

250g/8oz strong white flour
500g/1lb wholemeal flour
3 teaspoons salt
1 sachet (7g/¼oz) fast-action dried yeast
1 level tablespoon soft light brown sugar
450ml/15fl oz warm water
4 tablespoons vegetable oil

Mix both flours, the salt and dried yeast in a large bowl. Make a well in the centre. Mix the sugar with the water and pour into the well. Pour in the oil and blend all the ingredients together until you have a smooth elastic dough.

Turn the dough out on to a board and knead for 5 minutes. Put into a clean bowl, cover with a greased plastic bag and leave to prove in a warm place for 2 hours. The bowl with the dough can be stood in another, larger bowl filled with hot water, as a surefire way of keeping the dough warm: remember to change the water as it cools.

Turn out the dough and knead again to remove any air bubbles. Shape into 3 loaves and put on a greased baking tray. Cover, and leave to prove for a further 25 minutes until slightly puffy. Preheat the oven to 220°C/425°F/gas 7.

Bake the loaves in the preheated oven for 40 minutes, or until crusty on top. To check the bread is cooked through, tap the underneath of each loaf: it should sound hollow when cooked. Cool the loaves on a wire rack to allow the steam to escape and prevent the loaves from becoming damp.

WHOLEMEAL SHORTCRUST PASTRY

The wholemeal flour we buy from Dove's Farm, near Hunger-ford, comes from 100% organically grown wheat. The grain is stone-ground to preserve the valuable wheatgerm oil content. Pastry made from this wheat has a rich, nutty flavour and, of course, is healthier. This pastry freezes well in 250g/8oz portions.

MAKES 750 G/1½ LB

250g/8oz plain white flour
250g/8oz wholemeal flour
½ teaspoon salt
250g/8oz margarine (not a low-fat substitute)
about 300ml/10fl oz water

Mix the flours and salt together in a large bowl. Cut the margarine into small cubes and add to the flour. Rub the fat into the flour between fingers and thumb until there are no lumps of margarine and the mixture resembles fresh bread-crumbs. Pour in a little of the water and, using a round-bladed knife, stir until the mixture begins to stick together, gradually adding more water as required. Knead the mixture lightly for a few seconds until you have a firm, smooth dough. Allow to rest for about 15 minutes before using. The pastry can be wrapped in clingfilm and stored in the refrigerator for about 2 days.

When the pastry is required, remove from the refrigerator and allow to come to room temperature for at least 2 hours. Sprinkle a little flour on to a board and roll out the dough, turning occasionally until it is evenly rolled.

The usual baking temperature is a hot oven (220°C/425°F/gas 7), unless otherwise stated in the recipe.

CHEDDAR CHEESE PASTRY

This versatile cheese pastry has many uses: for flan cases, biscuits, and an unusual pie crust. We sometimes use it for enveloping a poached fillet of trout or salmon. For a first course, we make a soufflé of smoked goat's cheese and serve it in a tartlet case made with this cheese pastry (see page 154). Any leftover pastry can be made into small biscuits.

MAKES 300 G/10 OZ PASTRY, OR 6 × 7.5 CM/3 INCH FLANS

90g/3oz butter
90g/3oz Cheddar cheese, finely grated
125g/4oz plain flour
a few shakes of cayenne pepper
pinch of salt

Preheat the oven to 190°C/375°F/gas 5.

Cream the butter and grated cheese together until soft. Gradually work in the flour. Add the cayenne pepper and salt and mix thoroughly. Alternatively; put all the ingredients into a food processor and blend until the mixture sticks together.

Knead the cheese dough into a ball and allow to rest. Cool hands are best, and do not handle too much because in such a rich dough the butter may become oily.

Roll out the dough and cut circles the size of your flan tins. Press the pastry circles into the flan tins and chill in the refrigerator for at least 30 minutes before required (they can also be left much longer). Bake in the preheated oven for about 10 to 15 minutes until the pastry is golden.

Cook's note: The dough can be frozen, but it must be thawed gently and it must be at room temperature before rolling out.

CHOUX PASTRY

Choux pastry does not keep well, so make only as much as you need. It should be used within 3 hours of baking. This pastry is baked in a hot oven with a rising temperature: for 10 minutes at 200°C/400°F/gas 6, then for the remaining baking time at 220°C/425°F/gas 7, to ensure that the pastry is crisp and nicely browned. If still pale in colour, it will collapse when removed from the oven. Bake choux pastry on a dampened baking tray (hold the baking tray under cold running water for a couple of seconds). Once baked, take the pastries off the sheet to cool and cut with a sharp knife to allow the steam to escape and prevent sogginess.

SERVES 3 to 4

150ml/5fl oz water
60g/2oz butter
75g/2½oz plain flour
2 free-range eggs

Preheat the oven to 200°C/400°F/gas 6.

Put the water and butter into a fairly large saucepan. Sift the flour on to a piece of baking parchment. Bring the water in the pan to the boil and, when bubbling, draw aside. Once the bubbles have subsided tip in the flour and stir vigorously with a wooden spoon until the mixture is smooth. This should take a few seconds. Do not overbeat or the pastry will not rise.

Cool the mixture for 5 minutes, then beat in the eggs one at a time. If the eggs are large, break the last one into a bowl and beat separately with a fork, then pour it gradually into the mixture. The mixture should be firm and hold its shape, and you may not need to use all of the remaining egg.

Beat the dough for approximately 3 to 4 minutes until it looks glossy. Put into a piping bag with a plain éclair nozzle, or use a dessertspoon, and pipe or spoon the mixture on to the dampened baking tray in éclair or bun shapes. Bake in the preheated oven for 10 minutes, then turn up the temperature to 220°C/425°F/gas 7 and bake for a further 15 minutes.

Lift the pastries off the baking tray, cut them to release the steam and allow to cool.

8

Savoury and Sweet Sauces

MAYONNAISE

MAKES 180 ML/6 FL OZ

2 free-range egg yolks at room temperature
½ level teaspoon salt
¼ teaspoon freshly ground white pepper
½ teaspoon caster sugar
2 good teaspoons Dijon mustard
150ml/5fl oz vegetable or olive oil (or mixture of both)
2 tablespoons white wine vinegar or tarragon vinegar

Put the egg yolks into a basin with the salt, pepper, sugar and mustard.

Add the oil a little at a time, whisking in thoroughly as you go.

When the mixture begins to thicken a little, vinegar can be added to make whisking easier. When all the oil has been used up, gradually pour in the remaining vinegar.

BÉCHAMEL

A well-made sauce makes all the difference to the flavour and appearance of many dishes. Béchamel, made from a roux (the cooking together of melted butter or other fat and flour), is the foundation for a variety of sauces.

MAKES JUST OVER 300 ML/10 FL OZ

450ml/15fl oz milk
1 shallot or small onion, peeled and sliced
1 small carrot, peeled and chopped
1 small stick tender celery, chopped
4 peppercorns
1 small bay leaf
45g/1½oz unsalted butter
2½ tablespoons plain flour
sea salt and freshly ground black pepper

Put the milk, vegetables and flavourings into a pan and simmer for a couple of minutes until the vegetables are soft. Do not allow to boil over. Remove from the heat, cover and leave to infuse for about 15 minutes. Then strain off into a pan.

To make the roux: melt the butter in a pan, add the flour and stir with a wooden spoon until the mixture is smooth. Cook over a gentle heat for 2 to 3 minutes, stirring all the time until the mixture begins to bubble.

Remove the roux from the heat and gradually pour in the strained infused milk, stirring after each addition to prevent lumps from forming. Return to the heat and bring the sauce to the boil, stirring continuously. Once it has thickened, cook for a further 2 minutes. Season to taste.

There are three variations of roux: pouring consistency (as above), coating consistency and binding consistency.

FOR COATING CONSISTENCY:
45g/1½oz unsalted butter
45g/1½oz plain flour
sea salt and freshly ground black pepper
300ml/10fl oz milk and stock mixed

Make the sauce as above. All that has changed is the quantity of butter and flour.

FOR BINDING CONSISTENCY:
60g/2oz unsalted butter
60g/2oz plain flour
300ml/10fl oz milk and stock mixed
sea salt and freshly ground black pepper

This very thick sauce is used for binding mixtures, such as for croquettes.

Melt the butter and add the flour, stirring well. Cook gently for 3 minutes, stirring all the time until the roux begins to bubble and comes away from the sides of the pan. Gradually pour in the liquid and bring to the boil, stirring all the time. Cook for 2 minutes after it has thickened, then season to taste.

CHESHIRE (OR CHEDDAR) CHEESE SAUCE

Cheshire cheese is reputed to be the oldest cheese in Britain, made even before Roman times. You can use a blue-veined Cheshire or the more common red or white Cheshire. You can, of course, use Cheddar instead if you prefer, though you should choose a mild-flavoured one as the sauce should not overpower the main dish it accompanies.

SERVES 4

30g/1oz unsalted butter
30g/1oz plain flour
1 teaspoon English mustard
300ml/10fl oz full-cream milk
90g/3oz Cheshire cheese, grated
sea salt, cayenne and freshly ground white pepper to taste
90ml/3fl oz double cream

Melt the butter in a saucepan over a low heat. Stir in the flour and mustard and cook, stirring all the time, for about 1 minute until the mixture becomes lighter in colour. Remove the pan from the heat and pour in the milk, blending well together. Return the pan to the heat and bring to the boil to cook the flour. If the sauce still tastes floury it needs a little more cooking.

Remove from the heat and beat in the grated cheese. Season to taste with salt, cayenne and pepper. Beat in the double cream. Serve at once or keep warm in a saucepan over another saucepan of warm water (to prevent the cheese becoming overcooked).

ONION SAUCE

Reminiscent of Sunday lunches accompanied by *Family Favourites* on the radio. I wonder how many of us remember that programme, which played requests from and for emigrating families, sweethearts and service men and women all over the world. Angela had a request played on this programme back in 1971 when she was in Malta. Her mother requested Edith Piaf's 'No Regrets' but Angela could not hear the song properly because nearly everyone in the quarters was piling in to tell her she had just been mentioned on *Family Favourites*. Likewise in England, Angela's family did not hear much of the request either, because neighbours and friends called in or telephoned to see if they had the radio switched on. Angela's mother tells me that the lunch that Sunday was roast lamb with an onion sauce, but it was not quite the same as this recipe, the maker of sauces being away in Malta.

SERVES 4

60g / 2oz unsalted butter
2 large onions, peeled and thinly sliced
300ml / 10fl oz milk
1 tablespoon cornflour, slackened in 150ml / 5fl oz water
sea salt and freshly ground black pepper
120ml / 4fl oz double cream

Melt the butter in a saucepan and stir in the onion, covering well with the butter. Cover and cook until the onion is just softening. Pour in the milk and cook for a couple of minutes, then pour in the slackened cornflour and cook gently until the sauce has thickened. Season to taste and stir in the cream. If a smoother consistency is required, liquidize for a couple of minutes in a food processor or blender.

GREEN PEA AND
SPRING ONION SAUCE

A delicately flavoured sauce to accompany fish, such as the plaice
and spinach parcels on page 72.

SERVES 4 to 6

60g/2oz butter
4 spring onions, cut into small rings
350g/12oz shelled fresh green peas
150ml/5fl oz water
150ml/5fl oz milk
sea salt and freshly ground black pepper
2 teaspoons chopped fresh tarragon
150ml/5fl oz single cream

Melt the butter in a saucepan and lightly cook the spring onion
until just softening. Put in the peas, water and milk and bring to
simmering point. Cook for a few minutes until the peas are
tender. (If the peas are really fresh, just heating through will do.
Do not overcook them or they will lose their colour.) Add salt,
pepper and the tarragon. Transfer the mixture to a food processor
or blender and liquidize until smooth.

Just before serving, pour into a saucepan, stir in the cream, and
heat through but do not boil.

SPRING ONION AND TARRAGON SAUCE

Accompanies dishes such as vegetarian rissoles or croquettes. It is also excellent with poached white fish such as sole, plaice or whiting, and has the added beauty of being so quick and easy to make that you can put it together for a last-minute or unexpected guest when the sauces on the table have been finished.

SERVES 4

1 bunch spring onions (about 6 to 8)
30g/1oz unsalted butter
150ml/5fl oz milk
3 teaspoons cornflour, slackened in a little of the milk
150ml/5fl oz single cream
2 sprigs fresh tarragon, stalks removed, leaves chopped
sea salt and freshly ground black pepper

Cut the spring onions into small rings. Melt the butter in a saucepan and put in the onions. Cook gently until soft. Pour in the milk and the slackened cornflour and cook until the mixture has thickened. Pour in the cream, add the tarragon, season to taste, stir well to blend and keep the sauce warm until required.

SORREL OR SPINACH SAUCE

This is a very versatile sauce that goes with a variety of dishes, such as vegetable pies and rissoles, and white fish or chicken.

SERVES 4

1 small onion, peeled and finely chopped
60g/2oz unsalted butter
250g/8oz fresh sorrel or spinach leaves, washed and roughly chopped
225ml/8fl oz chicken or vegetable stock
150ml/5fl oz medium-dry white wine
1 teaspoon clear honey
4 tablespoons single cream
sea salt and freshly ground black pepper

Cook the onion in the butter until soft and very lightly browned, then add the sorrel or spinach and cook gently for about 10 minutes. Pour in the stock, wine and honey and bring to the boil.

Put the mixture into a blender and mix until you have a smooth purée. Return to a clean saucepan and gradually whisk in the cream. Season to taste and serve.

SPICY TOMATO SAUCE

Serves as an accompanying sauce or as a dip. It is particularly good with the Leicester doughnuts on page 36. This sauce also freezes well and is a good standby.

SERVES 4 to 6

4 tablespoons olive or vegetable oil
1 onion, peeled and finely chopped
1 clove garlic, crushed with a little salt
1kg/2lb ripe tomatoes, skinned (page 12), deseeded and chopped
1 tablespoon tomato purée
150ml/5fl oz chicken or vegetable stock
1 tablespoon chopped fresh parsley
2 teaspoons sugar
1 teaspoon fresh or dried oregano
1 teaspoon freshly ground white pepper
¼ teaspoon cayenne pepper
sea salt and freshly ground black pepper

Heat the oil gently in a saucepan. Add the onion and garlic and cook until just turning golden-brown. Stir in the tomatoes then add all the remaining ingredients and blend well together. Simmer for 45 minutes. The sauce can be liquidized at this stage if you prefer a smoother consistency. Check the seasonings and serve.

FRESH ORANGE SAUCE
FOR FISH

During the 1970s, when we had our outside catering company, it was *de rigueur* in country houses to serve soup, fish, meat, sweet, cheese and coffee for dinner, the order varying little. For the fish course, one of our favourites (because it could be prepared in advance and kept in the refrigerator until the last minute), and fortunately also a favourite of our clients, was a fresh fillet of plaice served with an orange sauce. It is very refreshing, particularly if the first course has been a spicy or thick soup. This sauce goes well with a variety of white fish dishes, such as quenelles (page 62) or whiting and plaice fillets. Use a good-flavoured medium-sweet wine. If the wine is too dry, the sauce can turn out to have a bitter taste. You may wish for an even sweeter-tasting sauce, in which case add a spoonful of clear honey when heating the sauce to serve.

SERVES 3 to 4

finely grated rind and juice of 1 small orange
finely grated rind and juice of 1 small lemon
120ml/4fl oz double cream
3 large free-range egg yolks
150ml/5fl oz full-bodied white wine such as a Chardonnay or fruity Alsace
a little cayenne pepper
sea salt and freshly ground black pepper
60g/2oz unsalted butter
2 tablespoons clear honey (optional)

Put the citrus juices (reserve the rind) into a bowl and stir in the cream, egg yolks and wine. At this stage, it may look as though the mixture is curdling and the cream separating. Do not worry, it all comes together during cooking.

Set the bowl over a saucepan of simmering water. Whisk continuously until the mixture has the consistency of thin cream. Season to taste with cayenne, salt and black pepper. Blend in the orange and lemon rind. Cut the butter into small pieces and beat them one by one into the sauce. Keep the sauce hot, but do not allow to boil. Add the honey at this stage, if used. Allow it to melt and blend in before spooning the sauce over the fish.

PLUM AND BRANDY SAUCE

This sauce is excellent with spiced Tudor lamb patties (page 98), along with many other dishes. Port can be used as an alternative to brandy; use double the quantity. When cooked, the sauce can be poured into a jar and refrigerated until required. It can also be mixed into game casseroles, or added to the pan juices of a roasting leg of lamb for a rich, delicious, plum gravy.

SERVES 6 to 8

120ml/4fl oz vegetable oil
1 medium onion, peeled and finely chopped
1 clove garlic, crushed with a little salt
750g/1½lb dark plums, stones removed
4 tablespoons brandy or 8 tablespoons (120ml/4fl oz) port
¼ teaspoon ground allspice
small sprig fresh rosemary
150ml/5fl oz dry white wine
150ml/5fl oz water
2 tablespoons redcurrant jelly

Pour the oil into a large saucepan, add the onion and cook until soft. Add the garlic and stir well together, then put in the plums, brandy or port, allspice and rosemary. Pour in the wine and water. Simmer gently until the plums are quite soft. Slow cooking concentrates the flavours and enriches the sauce.

Remove and discard the rosemary. Pour the sauce into a food processor or liquidizer, add the redcurrant jelly and blend until the mixture is smooth. Use as required.

SMOKED HAM SAUCE

Good with jacket potatoes, bacon and sorrel potato patties (page 38), or the potato and stilton croquettes on page 168, thereby making a vegetarian dish suitable for meat-eaters.

SERVES 3 to 4

30g/1oz unsalted butter
1 small clove garlic, crushed with a little salt
½ medium onion, peeled and very finely chopped
150ml/5fl oz milk
a very little salt and plenty of freshly ground black pepper
2 teaspoons cornflour, slackened in a little milk
4 tablespoons double cream
60g/2oz smoked ham, thinly sliced and cut into strips
bunch fresh chives, finely chopped

Put the butter into a saucepan and cook the garlic and onion together for a couple of minutes. Pour in the milk and add the seasoning: not too much salt because the ham will be slightly salty, but plenty of pepper. Pour in the slackened cornflour and stir to thicken and cook for a couple of minutes. Stir in the cream, then fold in the ham and chives, blend well together and serve.

DARK CHOCOLATE SAUCE

An amazingly simple sauce, quick to make and a perfect accompaniment for many puddings and ice creams. As a change from double cream we sometimes serve this with Connemara chocolate cake (page 214).

SERVES 4

125g/4oz dark chocolate
2 tablespoons caster sugar
1 teaspoon cocoa
1 teaspoon coffee essence (such as Camp)
300ml/10fl oz water
½ teaspoon vanilla extract

Break up the chocolate and put into a saucepan with all the other ingredients. Heat slowly, stirring frequently until dissolved. Simmer without a lid until the sauce has the consistency of cream.

TANGERINE SABAYON

The time taken to make a sabayon depends upon the thickness of the mixing bowl. A fairly thick bowl will take about 10 minutes to cook the sauce, while a thinner bowl will naturally require less time. A heatproof glass bowl is best: it enables you to check that the sabayon is not turning to scrambled egg at the bottom of the bowl. Sabayon must be whisked constantly. If the telephone or door bell rings, try to ignore it until the sabayon is ready, or shout loudly for assistance.

SERVES 4

finely grated rind and juice of 4 tangerines or satsumas
4 tablespoons icing sugar
4 tablespoons Grand Marnier or Cointreau
juice of 1 lemon
4 large free-range egg yolks
120ml / 4fl oz double cream

Put all the ingredients except the cream into a heatproof mixing bowl and stand the bowl over a saucepan of simmering water. Do not allow the base of the bowl to touch the water. Whisk until the eggs begin to thicken. When the sauce has thickened, blend in the cream. The sabayon is now ready to use.

WHISKY SABAYON

As well as accompanying the dark chocolate pudding on page 188 and the fresh pear and ginger crumble on page 180, this sauce is super with apple pie or crumble, mince pies, fresh fruit salad, and chocolate or vanilla ice cream. We also often pour the whisky sauce over hot bananas sautéed in butter and rum.

SERVES 4

4 tablespoons icing sugar
120ml / 4fl oz malt or single-blend whisky
juice of 1 lemon
4 large free-range egg yolks
120ml / 4fl oz single cream

Put all the ingredients except the cream into a heatproof mixing bowl and stand the bowl over a saucepan of simmering water. Do not allow the base of the bowl to touch the water. Whisk until the eggs begin to thicken. When the sauce has thickened, blend in the cream. The sabayon is now ready to use.

A fairly thick bowl will take about 10 minutes to cook the sauce, a thinner bowl less time.

9

Dressings and Preserves

NUT OIL DRESSING

SERVES 4

We make this dressing all the time and use it as a base, adding to it the extra ingredient that complements a particular salad.

1 small clove garlic, crushed with a little salt
4 tablespoons white wine vinegar
pinch of caster sugar
180ml/6fl oz hazelnut or walnut oil
180ml/6fl oz sunflower oil
2 tablespoons French mustard
juice of ½ lemon, or a little more if desired
2 tablespoons clear honey
sea salt and freshly ground black pepper

Put all the ingredients into a bowl and whisk well together. You can experiment with less or more garlic according to your taste.

STRAWBERRY VINAIGRETTE

This unusual dressing can be served with cold poached salmon or chicken or tossed into a cucumber and strawberry salad.

SERVES 4

60g/2oz strawberries, hulled
3 tablespoons strawberry or raspberry vinegar
2 tablespoons clear honey
juice of ½ lemon
180ml/6fl oz sunflower or grapeseed oil
sea salt and freshly ground black pepper

Put the strawberries into a food processor or blender with the vinegar, honey and lemon juice. Blend briefly until smooth. Put the purée through a sieve to remove any pips, then return the purée to the food processor or blender. With the machine running, gradually pour in the oil and blend until the mixture is smooth. Season well to taste.

MANGO VINAIGRETTE

This vinaigrette is ideal with smoked chicken, ham or smoked fish. A mango, orange and green leaves salad tossed in mango vinaigrette is colourful and delicious with many cold summer dishes.

SERVES 4

1 small, very ripe mango, peeled
3 tablespoons red wine vinegar
juice of ½ lemon
1 teaspoon French mustard
2 tablespoons clear honey
sea salt and freshly ground black pepper
150ml / 5fl oz sunflower oil
1 tablespoon finely chopped fresh parsley

Slice the mango flesh away from the stone. Put the flesh into a food processor or blender along with the vinegar, lemon juice, mustard, honey, salt and pepper. Blend until the mixture is smooth. Still blending, gradually pour in the oil until the mixture thickens slightly and has a smooth consistency. Pour into a jug, stir in the parsley and check the seasoning.

PEACH AND APPLE CHUTNEY

An excellent standby to have in your cupboard to accompany a variety of pâtés, cold meat and cheese. The skins are left on the peaches to give a good colour to the chutney.

MAKES 2.25 KG/5 LB

1.7 litres/3 pints water
750g/1½lb demerara sugar
600ml/1 pint white wine vinegar
1.25kg/2½lb fresh peaches, stones removed, chopped
750g/1½lb apples, peeled, cored and sliced
1 tablespoon salt
90g/3oz fresh root ginger, peeled and grated
4 cloves garlic, crushed with a little salt
2 teaspoons chilli powder
125g/4oz raisins
125g/4oz dried apricots, finely chopped
5cm/2-inch cinnamon stick

Pour the water into a preserving pan or large, heavy-based saucepan, add the sugar and vinegar and bring to the boil. Reduce the heat and stir until the sugar has dissolved. Add all the remaining ingredients and bring back to the boil, stirring from time to time. Reduce the heat and simmer until the liquid has reduced and the mixture has thickened. It should be thick enough so that a wooden spoon drawn across the base of the pan leaves a channel which does not close again.

Remove from the heat, remove the stick of cinnamon and allow the chutney to cool. Then pot and seal in clean jars in the usual way (see page xv).

AUTUMN HARVEST CHUTNEY

It is interesting how recipes sometimes evolve into something quite different from the original intention. This was originally a dark plum sauce but we found ourselves needing a tasty chutney to accompany a game pâté. Angela, for once, thought my suggestion of rearranging a dark plum sauce and adding a few other ingredients to make a plum chutney was a good idea, and it turned out to be a very delicious and different preserve. The blueberries are optional, but they do add to the flavour and colour. Serve the chutney with a variety of pâtés or cold meats. Especially good with the duck sausages on page 116.

MAKES 15–18 × 500 G/1 LB JARS

2.5kg/6lb dark plums, stones removed, chopped
1kg/2lb cooking apples, peeled, cored and chopped
6 red onions, peeled and chopped
500g/1lb blueberries (optional)
500g/1lb raisins
1kg/2lb soft dark brown sugar
4 teaspoons salt
2 teaspoons ground mixed spice
1 nutmeg, freshly grated
3 teaspoons ground ginger
2 teaspoons cayenne pepper
300ml/10fl oz sherry vinegar
1.1 litres/2 pints malt vinegar

Put the plums, apples, onion and blueberries, if using, into a large, heavy-based saucepan. Cook over a gentle heat until the juices begin to run, then add the raisins, sugar, salt, all the spices and both vinegars. Stir well to blend. Raise the heat slightly, and cook the chutney until the mixture has thickened and the liquid reduced. Stir from time to time to prevent sticking. A splash guard is helpful at this stage to protect yourself and your cooker from the deep red juices.

As soon as the chutney has thickened (so that a wooden spoon drawn across the base of the pan leaves a channel which does not close again), remove from the heat. The mixture will thicken a little more as it cools.

When the chutney has cooled, pot and seal in clean jars in the usual way (see page xv).

PINEAPPLE AND MINT JELLY

An unusual jelly, to go with the curried chicken and fruit salad on page 93. It also goes well with other cold dishes, such as ham mousse (page 26), or cold meats and salads. For the wine use a good, fruity Alsace, a Gewürztraminer, or an Australian Rosemount Chardonnay, full of ripe fruit flavours. Turn the jelly out of the mould and serve either whole with fresh pineapple in the centre, or cut the jelly into cubes and arrange around the chicken, mousse or meat as a garnish. If you are feeling creative, brush a few fresh mint leaves with a little oil and arrange around the inside of the mould before adding the second quantity of jelly liquid.

MAKES 1.1 LITRES/2 PINTS

600ml/1 pint pineapple juice
150ml/5fl oz good quality, fruity white wine
2 tablespoons lemon juice
juice of 2 oranges
1 small fresh pineapple, peeled and core removed
30g/1oz gelatine, soaked in 180ml/6fl oz water
2 tablespoons chopped fresh mint
fresh whole mint leaves for decoration

Put half the pineapple juice into a saucepan with the wine and lemon and orange juices. Put the remaining pineapple juice aside. Cut the pineapple into small cubes and put half into the saucepan with the liquid ingredients. Put the remaining pineapple to one side. Bring to the boil and cook the pineapple for about 2 minutes. This breaks down the enzymes in the pineapple that would otherwise prevent the jelly from setting.

Remove the saucepan from the heat and stir in the soaked gelatine. This must be blended in well. Pour in the reserved pineapple juice and stir round. This also helps to speed up the cooling process.

Pour 2.5cm/1 inch of liquid jelly into a 1.1-litre/2-pint ring mould, distributing evenly some of the pieces of cooked pineapple. Set aside a few pieces of cooked pineapple and the remainder of the jelly mixture (at room temperature) for the next stage. Put the mould into a bowl of ice cubes and cold water or put in the freezer to set for 15 to 20 minutes.

When set, remove the mould from the freezer or bowl of ice cubes and water. Arrange the remaining cooked pineapple around the mould on top of the set jelly. Stir 1 tablespoon of the mint into the remaining liquid jelly mixture, then top up the mould with it. Allow to set fully in the refrigerator for 2 to 3 hours.

When required, turn the jelly out by dipping the base of the mould into very hot water, quickly wiping the outside, placing a plate over the top of the jelly and inverting. The plate should now be on the bottom and the mould on top. Give a good sharp shake or two to release the jelly; it should come away easily. Lift off the mould.

Toss the remaining uncooked pineapple cubes with the remaining tablespoon of chopped mint and pile into the centre of the jelly. Arrange mint leaves around the top of the jelly ring.

APPLE MARMALADE

Firm, ripe eating apples are needed for this recipe. The marmalade can be potted and preserved in the same way as a jam. It is excellent for adding to pork or game casseroles, instead of the more usual redcurrant jelly, for a wonderfully rich stock. We have used it in the rabbit and cider casserole on page 122. As this is a preserve, it is a good way of using up a glut of apples. The sugar is measured against the quantity of apple purée, so cook the apples to a pulp before measuring quantities.

good-flavoured eating apples
500g/1lb granulated sugar to each 600ml/1 pint of apple purée: see note above

Wipe the apples clean and cut them into quarters. Do not peel or core. Put the apples into a preserving or very large, heavy-based saucepan with sufficient water to cover. Cook slowly over a low heat, stirring frequently, until they are reduced to a thick purée. Pass the purée through a sieve or vegetable mill.

Wash the pan the apples were cooked in. Measure the pulp and to each 600ml/1 pint pulp allow 500g/1lb sugar. Put the pulp and sugar into the pan and cook, stirring continuously, until it is of a jam-like consistency. It should be thick enough so that a wooden spoon drawn across the base of the pan leaves a channel which does not close again.

Pot and seal in clean jars in the usual way (see page xv).

Index